Building Museum Boards

Building Museum Boards

Third Edition

DARYL FISCHER AND LAURA B. ROBERTS

ROWMAN & LITTLEFIELD
Lanham • Boulder • New York • London

Published by Rowman & Littlefield
A wholly owned subsidiary of The Rowman & Littlefield Publishing Group, Inc.
4501 Forbes Boulevard, Suite 200, Lanham, Maryland 20706
www.rowman.com

Unit A, Whitacre Mews, 26-34 Stannary Street, London SE11 4AB

British Library Cataloguing in Publication Information Available

Library of Congress Cataloging-in-Publication Data Available

ISBN 978-1-5381-0843-7 (pbk. : alk. paper)
ISBN 978-1-5381-0844-4 (electronic)

∞™ The paper used in this publication meets the minimum requirements of American National Standard for Information Sciences—Permanence of Paper for Printed Library Materials, ANSI/NISO Z39.48-1992.

Printed in the United States of America

Contents

Foreword   vii

About Templates for Trustees   ix

Using the Templates for Trustees *Online App*   xi

Building Museum Boards *User's Guide*   xxi

Acknowledgments   xxiii

Introduction: Best Practices in Museum Governance   1
    Mission Matters   1
    The Governance Committee   1
    Fundamental Board Duties   2
    Term Limits   3
    Different Kinds of Diversity   3
    Advisory Boards   5
    More Productive Meetings   5
    Use of Executive Session   7

1   Understanding the Nominations Cycle   9
    Template 1: Nominations Timeline (Figures 1.1–1.4)   9

2   Gathering Feedback from Current Board Members   13
    Template 2: Individual Board Member Profile   13
    Full Participation Counts   13
    Customizing the Template   13
    Why Does Personality Matter?   14
    A Balanced Board   14
    Report 2: Board Profile Summary and Graphs (Figures 2.1–2.8)   17

3   Identifying New Board Prospects   23
    Recommending Prospects   23
    Tracking the Recruitment Process   23
    Template 3: Board Prospects (Figures 3.1–3.2)   24

4 Clarifying Board Roles   27

    Template 4: Board and Officer Job Descriptions   28

5 Delineating Committees and Task Forces   31

    Standing Committees or Task Forces?   31

        Template 5: Board Committee and Task Force Charters   33

6 Securing Commitments from Board Members   35

    Board Contract   35

        Template 6A: Board Contract   36

    Conflict of Interest Policy and Disclosure Statement   38

        Template 6B: Conflict of Interest Policy   39

        Template 6C: Conflict of Interest Disclosure Form   42

    Not for New Trustees Alone   44

7 Assessing the Process   45

        Template 7: First-Year Board Member Assessment Survey   46

        Report 7: First-Year Assessment (Figures 7.1–7.7)   47

8 Orienting New Board Members   51

    The Cornerstone of Board Development   51

        Template 8: Orientation (Figure 8.1)   53

    Mentors   56

    From Orientation to Activation   56

    Provide Other Resources   57

Resource Guide for Building Museum Boards   59

Appendix: Standing Committees and Ad Hoc Task Forces—Sample Purposes and Responsibilities   61

About the Museum Trustee Association and the Authors   65

Foreword

Thank you for your purchase of *Building Museum Boards*. Since its founding, the Museum Trustee Association (MTA) has communicated strategies and best practices to museums across the Americas. We are especially proud of this latest edition of our *Templates for Trustees* series, which digs deeper into trusteeship than ever before and provides the tools for an institution of any size to build, educate, and inspire a successful board.

Throughout the following pages are guidelines and best practices from industry leaders, both staff and volunteers. You will also find eight customizable and automated templates to help you keep your board organized and focused on the key issues and challenges facing your museum today. MTA staff is available to you for support as you work your way through the software.

MTA is the network for informing, advising, and inspiring museum trustees. For more information on our products, publications, and services, visit us at www.museumtrustee.org or call our offices. We look forward to hearing from you!

Richard Kelly
Board Chairman
Museum Trustee Association

Mary Baily Wieler
President
Museum Trustee Association

About *Templates for Trustees*

"When it comes to board information," says Harvard University professor Richard Chait, "less is more, and much less is much more."[1] Trustees usually receive too much information with too little meaning. Instead, they need structured, concise materials that enhance board performance and satisfaction while directing their attention to what matters most.

Templates for Trustees is a four-part series designed by the Museum Trustee Association (MTA) to focus attention on key processes and tasks of governance. It supports the MTA's mission "to enhance the effectiveness of museum trustees" by

- promoting and facilitating dialogue between museum trustees and museum directors
- collecting and disseminating information on museum governance that will assist trustees in discharging their responsibilities more effectively
- providing education and training opportunities for museum trustees
- initiating and conducting research on issues of concern to museum trustees

The templates are tools that present board information so that it can be collected, explored, and understood from different perspectives. Each one helps boards create documents, spreadsheets, and presentations tailored to their own needs. Using fill-in-the-blank forms, surveys, and rating scales that are provided on a unique cloud-based app, trustees or administrators enter specific information about their museum and their board. The completed templates and reports serve as starting points to help boards organize their thoughts, identify their priorities, and plan their actions.

Building Museum Boards is the first volume in the series. The other volumes include *The Leadership Partnership* (volume 2), *Executive Transitions* (volume 3), and *Strategic Thinking and Planning* (volume 4). All books in the series are available on a web-based application that is accessible to both PC and Mac users.

All four volumes have five sections:

- **Using the *Templates for Trustees* Online App** provides an overview of how the website is structured and a brief description of the purpose and functionality of each template and report. Specific instructions for working with the document library and web-based forms and customizing the templates for each museum's needs are available on the website. This online **Help Manual** will be useful to the administrator—the staff or the board member who will modify the forms so they are tailored to individual boards.

- The **User's Guide** goes through each of the templates and includes helpful nuts-and-bolts suggestions for how and when to distribute materials, how to interpret the graphs and charts, and how to present the slide shows. These will be useful to the Governance Committee, particularly the chair, or whoever will facilitate the process.
- A summary of relevant issues and trends, **Best Practices in Museum Governance**, sets the stage for the work.
- **Chapters 1 through 8** discuss the templates more fully and present examples of filled-in templates from hypothetical boards.
- The **Resource Guide** includes publications and organizations with additional information on board development.

TERMINOLOGY

In these volumes we have used the following terms:

- *Template library* includes the complete set of tools: surveys, database forms, documents, calendars, and presentations.
- *Template* refers to any tool that is modified by the administrator and filled out by board members.
- *Reports* are generated by compiling the responses to completed templates.
- *Trustee* refers to a member of the museum's governing board. We use the terms *board member* and *trustee* interchangeably throughout this manual.
- *Director* is the staff leader who reports to the board. Some museums may use *executive director, chief executive officer (CEO),* or *president.*
- *Board chair* is the senior board member who oversees all board functions. Some boards may use *chief volunteer officer (CVO)* or *president.*
- *Administrator* is the individual—typically a staff member in the executive office—who facilitates the governance assessment process and modifies and manages the templates.
- *Governance Committee* is the standing committee charged with generating and maintaining a healthy board. It may also be referred to as the *Nominating Committee,* the *Board Development Committee,* or the *Governance and Board Development Committee.*

TEMPLATE SUPPORT

The Museum Trustee Association provides support to boards that purchase *Templates for Trustees.* Please contact the MTA at Support@MuseumTrusteeTemplates.org

- for more information or to order additional volumes in the series
- with questions about tailoring or troubleshooting your templates (service included in the one-time setup fee)
- if you would like to make a testimonial about your experience using this or other volumes in the *Templates for Trustees* series

NOTE

1. Chait made this observation during a panel on "The New Work of the Nonprofit Board" at the American Association of Museums Annual Meeting in Baltimore, Maryland, April 2000.

Using the *Templates for Trustees* Online App

The physical book you are holding in your hands is just one part of *Building Museum Boards*. The templates themselves, which can be tailored to your institution, are stored in an online application hosted by the Museum Trustee Association (MTA). To activate your account in the application, you will need to contact the MTA at support@ museumtrusteetemplates.org, pay a modest one-time setup fee (waived for MTA members), and schedule a time to set up your account. Once you create an account, you can begin to review and customize the eight templates in *Building Museum Boards*. For example, once you have administered the surveys (Templates 2 and 7), you can generate Report 2, the graphs for Reports 2A–2M, and Report 7 and create the new board member orientation presentation (Template 8).

Throughout *Building Museum Boards* and the other books in the series, there is an important role for the "administrator" who manages the museum's use of the online application. In a larger museum, there may be someone who already manages board communication as part of his or her job. In a smaller museum, the administrator may be the director or a board member. It is also possible for two people to share that role. Once you have identified the individual who will fill that role, he or she should set up the application.

INITIAL SETUP

Step one is registering your account with the Museum Trustee Association by sending an email to support@ museumtrusteetemplates.org. The MTA staff member responsible for administering *Templates for Trustees* will send the administrator a short version of your museum's name (Museum ID), the administrator's user name, and a password, which will ensure the privacy and security of your museum's information. The staff person will also schedule a telephone call to go through the rest of the setup process.

Step two is logging into the application at www.museumtrusteetemplates.org. The first screen (figure 0.1) is the *Templates for Trustees* landing page, with general information about the MTA.

From there, click "Log in" on the blue bar to continue. Enter the information provided by MTA (figure 0.2).

After logging in, you will be on the landing page for the four volumes in *Templates for Trustees* (figure 0.3).

Step three: Before setting up any single volume, the administrator should establish the global settings. This will enable the application to customize the templates (figure 0.4). Click on "Settings" to launch the page with the placeholder settings. For each item in Settings—the museum name, mission statement, director's name, the title used by the director, and the first month of the museum's fiscal year, annual meeting, or the start of the board cycle—click on "Edit" and put the appropriate information in the field labeled "Setting Value." Click "Save," and you will be returned to the list of Settings. *Note:* You will not see the changes immediately. Close this menu, reopen Settings, and you will see the changes.

FIGURE 0.1
MTA *Templates for Trustees* Home Page (Courtesy of the Museum Trustee Association)

FIGURE 0.2
MTA *Templates for Trustees* Log In (Courtesy of the Museum
Trustee Association)

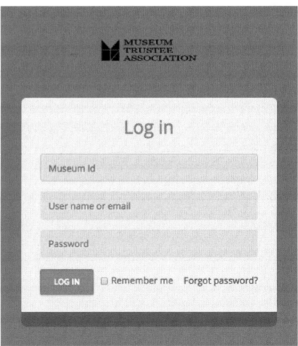

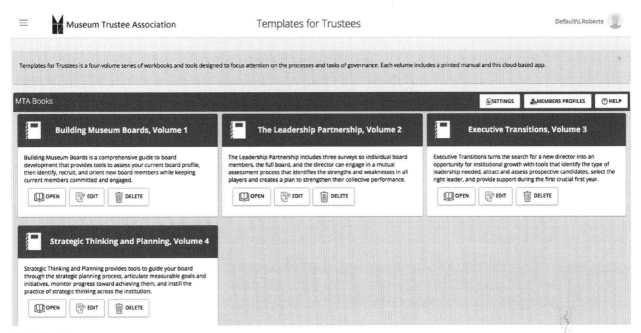

FIGURE 0.3
MTA *Templates for Trustees* Four Volumes Landing Page (Courtesy of the Museum Trustee Association)

For the Settings menu and most of the screenshots that follow, the information is for a fictitious museum—the Greenville Museum of Art and History—and its board.

Step four is creating a *Templates for Trustees* user account for everyone currently on the board, the director, and the administrator. Next to the MTA logo is a three-bar icon that opens the "Administration" menu (figure 0.5). Click that, and a new column will open on the left side with an arrow next to "Administration" (figure 0.6). Click on the arrow to open the menu and select "Users" (figure 0.7).

Click on the blue "Create New User" box (figure 0.8).

Settings/Placeholders

		ADD
Description	**Value**	
The title used by the director	Executive Director	EDIT · DELETE
The director's name	Jordan Charles	EDIT · DELETE
The museum's mission statement	Greenville Museum of Art and History broadens and deepens the community's connections to the heritage and culture of the region.	EDIT · DELETE
Month of the annual meeting and board elections	January	EDIT · DELETE
The name of the museum	Greenville Museum of Art and History	EDIT · DELETE

CLOSE

FIGURE 0.4
MTA *Templates for Trustees* Global Settings (Courtesy of the Museum Trustee Association)

FIGURE 0.5
Building Museum Boards Administration Menu Opener (Courtesy of the Museum Trustee Association)

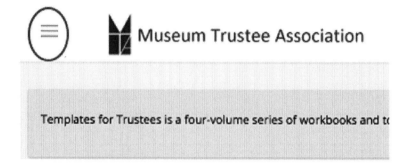

FIGURE 0.6
Building Museum Boards Administration Menu Selections (Courtesy of the Museum Trustee Association)

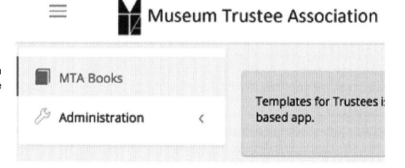

FIGURE 0.7
Building Museum Boards Administration Menu Selector (Courtesy of the Museum Trustee Association)

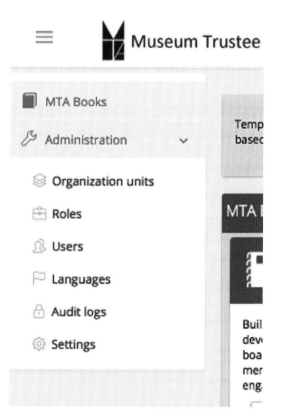

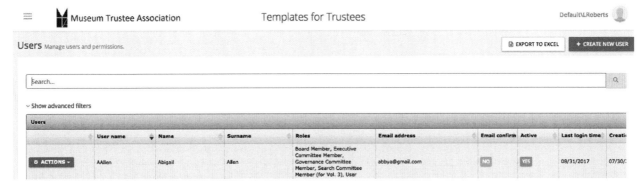

FIGURE 0.8
Building Museum Boards New User Setup (Courtesy of the Museum Trustee Association)

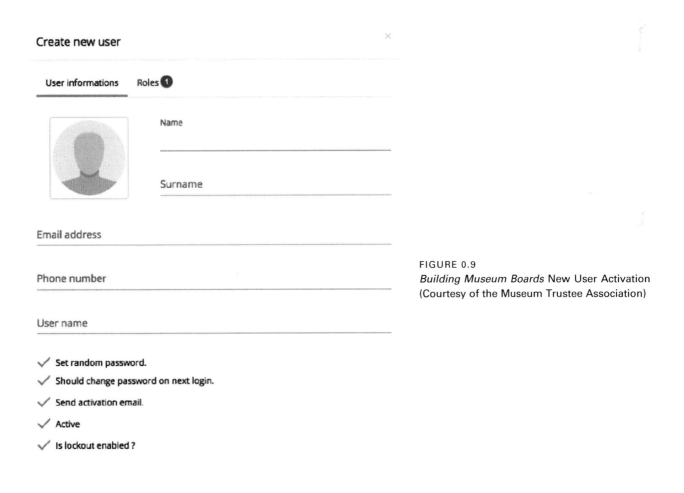

FIGURE 0.9
Building Museum Boards New User Activation (Courtesy of the Museum Trustee Association)

A window will pop up (figure 0.9) where you can enter basic information for each member of the board: name, email address, and a username. We suggest deciding on a convention for creating usernames: *first initial last name* is common. Note that the system will automatically send the new user an email with instructions for choosing a personal password.

Every user has one or more "roles" that determine their access to various features. In general, the roles are members and chair of the relevant committee (for this template, the Governance Committee), board members, Executive Committee members, board chair, executive director, and administrator. Just above the user's name, you will see "Roles" and a number in a blue circle. At first, that number will be "1" for the basic role of User. To add roles, click that circle. A menu of further roles opens; check all roles that user has and save (figure 0.10).

Because each of the roles will have different needs for information, there are different levels of access to templates and reports. Aside from the administrator, the chair of the Governance Committee will have the most extensive access to the files in this volume. Members of the Governance Committee will have greater access than other members of the board so that they can do the work of the committee. (Please note: Because this list of users is accessed by all of the *Templates for Trustees*, there are roles that are not relevant to *Building Museum Boards*. The administrator can add those roles when setting up other volumes.)

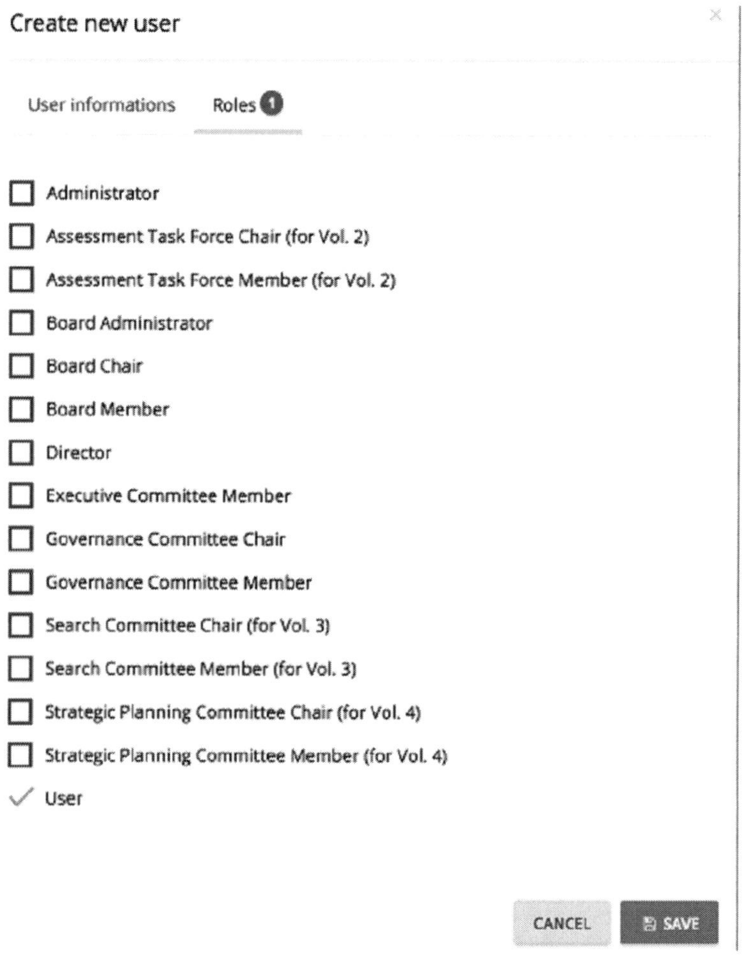

Create new user   ×

User informations   Roles **1**

☐ Administrator

☐ Assessment Task Force Chair (for Vol. 2)

☐ Assessment Task Force Member (for Vol. 2)

☐ Board Administrator

☐ Board Chair

☐ Board Member

☐ Director

☐ Executive Committee Member

☐ Governance Committee Chair

☐ Governance Committee Member

☐ Search Committee Chair (for Vol. 3)

☐ Search Committee Member (for Vol. 3)

☐ Strategic Planning Committee Chair (for Vol. 4)

☐ Strategic Planning Committee Member (for Vol. 4)

✓ User

CANCEL   🖫 SAVE

FIGURE 0.10
Building Museum Boards User Roles (Courtesy of the Museum Trustee Association)

FIGURE 0.11
Building Museum Boards User Edits (Courtesy of the Museum Trustee Association)

All of the users are entered into a table for further customizing and editing (figure 0.11). Click the blue "Actions" button next to the user's name and select "Edit." There is also a button that allows the administrator to "Create New User," which brings up the same screen shown in figure 0.9.

Every user must have an email address associated with their user profile. If one or more board members do not use email, we suggest setting up an account on the museum's email system, with mail forwarded to the administrator. That way, whenever an email is generated for the board member(s), the administrator will receive the intended survey, report, form, or document and can print a hard copy to send to the board member(s) by mail or arrange for it to be picked up at the museum.

Step five: Having set up all of the museum's users, it is time to start using the templates. Return to the three-bar menu next to the MTA logo and select "MTA Books" (figure 0.12), which will bring you back to the landing page for the four volumes in *Templates for Trustees*. Having purchased *Building Museum Boards*, that publication will be live.

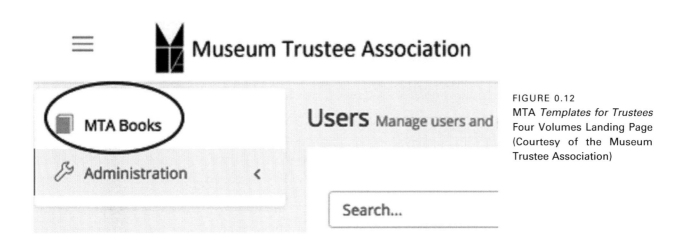

FIGURE 0.12
MTA *Templates for Trustees* Four Volumes Landing Page (Courtesy of the Museum Trustee Association)

FIGURE 0.13
Templates for Trustees Help Button (Courtesy of the Museum Trustee Association)

In addition to these basic instructions, *Templates for Trustees* has an online Help function with more detailed and specific instructions. The "Help" button is always on the blue bar, next to "Settings" and "Members Profiles" (figure 0.13).

Many truisms about museum recruitment warrant rethinking. The following quiz may shed new light on some old assumptions.

True or False?

1. Board recruitment and nominations activities are concentrated in the final months of the fiscal year so new trustees can be introduced at your annual meeting.

2. A few well-connected individuals can make contacts with all of the movers and shakers in your community.

3. Board recruitment and nominations is an ongoing process that requires sustained effort throughout the year.

4. Identification of candidates with the appropriate mix of skills, background, and experience is the job of the Governance Committee.

5. Board building is a process that requires the same kind of strategic thinking as other areas of board planning.

6. Orientation of new board members is best accomplished in a meeting in the first month of your fiscal year.

7. Board development opportunities such as special-focus board meetings and outside speakers are primarily for the benefit of new trustees.

8. Orientation of new board members is an ongoing process that provides opportunities for new board members to get involved and learn by doing.

Answers

1. *False.* Board building is not a seasonal activity that results in a flurry of activity leading up to your annual meeting. It is an ongoing process that lasts all year long.

2. *False.* Recruitment requires input from a large group of board and community members. In most communities, the same people are asked to serve on many boards. To find new leadership, you need to seek input from a wide spectrum of individuals.

3. *True.* It takes careful planning over many months to identify the skills and experience needed on your board, find people who possess them, introduce them to your museum, get their commitment, welcome them, and orient them.

4. *False.* The Governance Committee takes the lead in identifying board needs and initiates a discussion with the full board and others in the community, drawing suggestions from as many sources as possible.

5. *True.* Building a board requires clear and specific goals based on an understanding of your museum's current situation and a vision of its future. As boards think more strategically about nominations, recruitment, and orientation, they will spend more time planning for board development.

6. *False.* Orientation is an ongoing process that begins with the orientation session and continues throughout the year in relationships with mentors, appropriate board assignments, and ongoing board education.

7. *False.* Most board members are eager for opportunities to add to their skills and renew their commitment to the museum. Board development benefits new and veteran trustees alike.

8. *True.* The sooner new board members can get involved in appropriate assignments and ongoing board activities, the better.

Building Museum Boards User's Guide

Museum boards, directors, and governance gurus are increasingly aware of the importance of recruiting, orienting, and engaging board members. That's because an informed, involved, and committed board is among a museum's most valuable assets. Building this kind of board requires strategic thinking and planning and a long-term investment of time and energy. This effort pays big dividends for the museum and for the communities it serves.

The right tools make it easy to complete a job. Like a toolbox, this set of templates contains a selection of instruments that will help you accomplish specific tasks throughout the board-building process. They provide practical solutions to many of the challenges faced by those charged with identifying board needs, recruiting new board members to fill those needs, and orienting them so they can begin serving effectively.

Building Museum Boards includes eight templates.

Template 1: Nominations Timeline is a sequence of board-building steps tied to the start of your museum's board-building cycle: the museum's annual meeting, fiscal year, or calendar year. This timeline can serve as the Governance Committee's guide to the year's activities.

Template 2: Individual Board Member Profile is used to gather information from individual board members. That information is collected in **Report 2: Board Profile Summary**, a spreadsheet of all responses, and **Reports 2A–2M**, graphs that provide clear pictures of the board as a whole and each class of board members from many perspectives, such as demographics, experience, levels of giving, and personality styles.

Template 3: Board Prospects helps the Governance Committee monitor its progress in identifying, contacting, and recruiting nominees.

Template 4: Board and Officer Job Descriptions lists typical board responsibilities to clarify expectations for current and future board members.

Template 5: Committee and Task Force Charters provides a standard format for all committees and task forces. Typical descriptions of the most common museum board committees can be found on pages 61–63 of the appendix.

Template 6: Board Contract and Conflict of Interest Disclosure Form includes three documents. Template 6A outlines the mutual responsibilities of trustees and the museum in a Board Contract. This document will be tailored to the individual museum before it is printed and signed by the new board member and the museum director. There is also a standard Conflict of Interest Policy, which should be modified for your museum. Template 6B is a Disclosure Statement that will be distributed to all members for completion annually.

Template 7: First-Year Board Member Assessment is a survey that new board members complete at the end of their first year of service. The Governance Committee will use it to plan future recruitment and orientation. **Report 7**, generated by the online app, tabulates the responses.

Template 8: Orientation is a presentation to guide board orientation sessions. By inserting a variety of information about the museum, the Governance Committee can create a customized slide show.

Acknowledgments

John Adkins's thirty years of experience with technology includes writing apps for Fortune 500 companies. His knowledge and experience helped move *Templates for Trustees* into the twenty-first century with the introduction of the online app that is an integral part of each volume in this series. We are grateful for his creativity and persistence, which met every challenge we encountered in implementing this new platform.

The Museum Trustee Association and the authors thank Barbara Booker, coauthor of earlier editions of *Building Museum Boards*, and the dedicated group of advisors who contributed to that publication. We also thank Cinnamon Catlin-Legutko, Margaret Kadoyama, Margaret Middleton, and Lisa Watt for their advice about diversifying boards.

The Institute of Library and Museum Services generously supported earlier editions in the *Templates for Trustees* series.

The Museum Trustee Association gratefully acknowledges the following donors whose support made this series possible:

The Wieler Family Foundation in honor of Mary Baily Wieler and Emily Inglis
Georgina T. and Thomas A. Russo
Margaret and Bill Benjamin
Andrew L. and Gayle Shaw Camden
Richard and Mary Kelly
Maureen Pecht King
Janis and William Wetsman Foundation
Kristine and Leland Peterson
Katherine Duff Rines

Introduction

Best Practices in Museum Governance

MISSION MATTERS

Mission is the touchstone for all board activities, especially recruitment, orientation, and activation. One trustee put it this way: "The more affinity board members feel to your mission, the harder they'll work for you." A written mission statement is one of five policies/plans the American Alliance of Museums has designated as Core Documents. According to *Museum Board Leadership 2017*, a study undertaken by BoardSource for the American Alliance of Museums (AAM), "A good mission statement serves to guide organizational planning, board and staff decisions about programs and services, and priorities among competing demands for resources."[1] For all of these reasons, the museum's mission statement is included on many of the templates.

THE GOVERNANCE COMMITTEE

The group that is responsible for the health and well-being of the board—whether it is called the Nominating Committee, the Governance Committee, or the Board Development Committee—is arguably the most important committee of the board. In this manual and set of templates, we will use the term Governance Committee. This committee is responsible not only for bringing new members on board and making the best use of their knowledge, skills, and experience but also for keeping current board members actively engaged and helping them renew their commitment to the museum.

Given the Governance Committee's vital duties, its members should be chosen carefully by the board chair and the director. Committee members must have a clear understanding of the museum's mission, a vision of its future, an appreciation of the skills and experience of current board members, and a broad network of connections to the museum's many constituencies. The committee should draw on the knowledge and experience of people who are not board members, including individuals connected to the community through business, leadership programs, neighborhood associations, religious organizations, and schools. It should also look to staff members who may know individuals who have demonstrated a strong commitment to the museum by their behavior, such as donating to the collection, bringing fresh ideas, forming partnerships, and acting as advocates and bridge builders, as well as financial donors.

The Governance Committee should be aware of current and emerging practices in nonprofit governance as well as how museum boards compare with other nonprofits. For example, museum boards tend to be larger, with the average size being 17.7 members, as compared to 14.6 members for other nonprofits.[2] Larger boards may be recruited in hopes of increased fundraising capacity; however, large boards make it difficult to ensure that every member is meaningfully engaged in governance. The Governance Committee should stay abreast of the many relevant print and online resources, such as those included in the **Resource Guide** (pages 59–60), and bring relevant materials and professional development opportunities to the attention of the full board.

FUNDAMENTAL BOARD DUTIES

Nonprofit boards have three essential duties: the duty of care, the duty of obedience, and the duty of loyalty. These are not only principles of good governance but also legal standards to which all board actions are held. As the fiduciary body for a nonprofit museum, the board is responsible for the prudent stewardship of all of its assets (duty of care), ensuring that those assets are used to advance the museum's mission (duty of obedience), and ensuring that individual board members put the interests of the museum ahead of any personal or professional interests (duty of loyalty).

The board is also ultimately responsible for compliance with all local, state, and federal laws. The board should verify that all filing requirements and tax obligations are met. The organization must fill out IRS Form 990 completely, file it on time, and make it available to the public (generally done through posting on Guidestar.org, a database of more than two million nonprofit organizations recognized by the IRS). Filing Form 990 is no longer a task strictly for accountants, and the revised Form 990 demands that the board demonstrate a more thorough understanding of how the nonprofit functions. The board also ensures that the museum regularly withholds and pays employment taxes and documents and justifies the compensation of the executive director. All of this is part of the duty of care.

As part of the duty of loyalty, board members must intentionally avoid any conflicts of interest and refrain from participating in decisions that might benefit themselves, their business interests, or their immediate families. Every museum should have a conflict of interest policy that includes definition of interest, duty to disclose, and disclosure statements (filled out by all new board members and updated annually), guidelines for determining whether a conflict exists, procedures for addressing conflict, and processes for handling violations. It is often the responsibility of the Governance Committee to deal with such issues when they are reported. (See **Template 6: Board Contract and Conflict of Interest Disclosure Form**.)

These duties apply to all nonprofit boards. Museum boards should also be aware of the standards of museum ethics and approve an institutional code of ethics consistent with professional standards that applies to staff, board, and other volunteers.

State laws govern the bylaws of nonprofit organizations, but each board is responsible for adopting rules that specify the overall structure and operations of the museum. Issues addressed in the bylaws typically include:

- Name of museum
- Purpose
- Membership
- Minimum/maximum number of board members
- Number required for a quorum
- Terms and term limits
- Indemnification
- Officers
- Committees
- Meetings—regular, annual, and special
- Confidentiality
- Conflict of interest policy

- Code of ethics
- Records
- Amendments

Bylaws should be reviewed and revised periodically to allow for amendments such as email voting, meeting by telephone, or video conferencing.

TERM LIMITS

Whether board members should have term limits or be allowed to serve as long as they are willing and able is a question that has been debated for decades. The answer is yes. And yes. In general, term limits are best practice for most boards because they guarantee a regular infusion of new blood, fresh perspectives, alternative insights, and new faces around the board table. Term limits also provide a moment in time when the Governance Committee and board members can reevaluate their effectiveness and their commitment to the institution. Staggering terms has the added benefit of a steady influx of new board members without a mass exodus at any one point in time. The *Museum Board Leadership 2017* survey revealed that 66 percent of museum boards have some type of term limits.[3] The length and number of terms varies widely from one institution to another. Three-year terms are typical; however, terms can be as short as two years and as long as four years. Given that it takes at least a year for most new board members to learn the ropes, they're probably just starting to make valuable contributions in their second year, so it would be a poor investment of time for them to step down then. Regarding number of terms, two to four is typical. Some boards allow valuable members to step down for a year or two after completing their terms and then rejoin.

There are also boards (one-third of the respondents to *Museum Board Leadership 2017*) that choose not to have term limits for a variety of reasons. One is the expectation that board members are among the museum's largest contributors. If someone is giving large amounts of money or valuable collections, why would the museum want to lose them? Some boards fear that it might be awkward or seem ungrateful to ask a major donor to step down, even after a decade or more of board service. Smaller communities, where the pool of qualified and interested board members may be limited, may also be less inclined to have term limits.

Longtime board members may fear a lack of continuity, believing that they have the most in-depth knowledge of the institution and are responsible for maintaining its traditions and culture. At the same time, they may no longer have the energy for regular, active participation in monthly board meetings. If this is the case, they may appreciate the opportunity to serve on an advisory board or continue as ex officio members of board committees. Boards use the status of "honorary," "life," or "emeritus" to keep experienced trustees involved but no longer part of the voting governing board.

DIFFERENT KINDS OF DIVERSITY

Museums (and all nonprofits) have become acutely aware that diversity along many dimensions strengthens the board's capacity to be effective and responsible stewards and to realize their mission and vision. *Museum Board Leadership 2017* reports that nearly half (46 percent) of museum boards are all white, compared with 30 percent of other nonprofit boards. And while 56 percent of respondents agreed that "it is important to advance the level of board diversity and incorporate diversity into the organization's core values," only 10 percent said their board had a plan of action or allocated resources toward becoming more inclusive.[4]

While organizations rightly rely on the capacity and generosity of their boards, the Governance Committee should look beyond prospective members' ability to make financial contributions and consider those who bring perspective, expertise, and life experiences that are valuable to the museum. Understanding *all* of the value someone brings to the table, which requires a flexible way to calculate individual contributions, is key to achieving diversity. Younger people, those in education and other relevant professions, leaders of community nonprofits, and people with disabilities have great potential to contribute valuable perspectives. These board members can help the museum steward its social capital—a resource now recognized as equal in importance to financial capital.

Recruiting a demographically diverse board isn't easy, in part because the issues it involves—race, ethnicity, gender, and sexual orientation—are uncomfortable for many people to bring up, let alone address openly. And even when boards are willing to address these issues, they often don't know where to start because 91 percent of white Americans' social networks are made up of other white Americans.[5] But it is necessary because the more diverse perspectives are reflected on your board, the more strategically it can function. This is not new information. For decades, museums have been aware of the need to diversify their boards, staffs, and volunteers in order to advance their missions, broaden their base of support, and contribute to their communities. But progress has been slow and sporadic. In order to finally move the needle, boards can play a vital role in coming to understand and recognize how deep-seated racism and homophobia have prevented America's museums from serving its diverse citizenry.[6]

Bring your whole board together for a dialogue about these challenges, perhaps with the help of a facilitator who specializes in equity and inclusion. Come to consensus on your goals for diversifying your board before starting to identify potential new members. The *why* needs to come before the *who* so resist the temptation to go around the table and ask, "Who do we know?" Starting with people that current board members already know establishes a very small pool from which to recruit—a pool that is unlikely to include people with genuinely different backgrounds and perspectives. Instead, try this approach from *Blue Avocado* for getting beyond the usual suspects:

> Convene a "One-Meeting, Blue Ribbon Nominating Committee." Draw up a list of twenty well-connected people you would want on the board, but who you suspect wouldn't join. Examples might be funders, community leaders, and nonprofit executives. Invite them to come to a one-time meeting over lunch where they'll learn about the organization and what you're seeking in board members. Explain the mission, core programs and services, and reasons why your organization is seeking to diversify. Be explicit about what you're looking for people to *do* (rather than be). Then ask each person to suggest three individuals. The next day, call up the nominees and begin by explaining who referred them to you.[7]

To identify and recruit strong leadership from diverse communities that are new to the museum, don't rely on the people who are most visible to outsiders. Keep asking who really knows and understands the communities you would like to work with until you have found knowledgeable and well-connected individuals. You may want to consider adding non-board members to the Governance Committee so that their wider perspectives and networks are available to the committee throughout the year. Check your bylaws; non-board members may officially have to be guests of the Governance Committee. After a few cycles, if the experience has been positive, you may consider amending the bylaws to allow for full participation by non-board members.

As you start to identify potential new members, think in terms of constituencies rather than individuals. There are many different needs, interests, and views within any community—far more than a single person can represent—so look for a critical mass of two or three people from each of the communities you aim to serve better. This will take the pressure off individuals who are new to your board and expand the board's awareness of the different perspectives within each community, which is the basis for forming mutually rewarding relationships. Diversifying a board is hard work. The Governance Committee should be determined and persistent and continue to think about various dimensions of diversity in every cycle.

ADVISORY BOARDS

Some museums are embedded in or controlled by other entities, such as municipalities, colleges and universities, faith communities, and other nonprofits. In these cases, the board is strictly advisory and the fiduciary responsibility sits with either the government entity or the larger nonprofit. Clarity around the responsibilities and authority of advisory boards is essential. Common areas of potential conflict or uncertainty revolve around the process and procedures for appointing or electing members, policies regarding use of the facilities by partisan groups or candidates, solicitation and recognition of donors and sponsors, and intellectual freedom and integrity of research.

Stewardship of the collection is a particular area of concern. This is where advisory boards can provide a valuable service, helping the governing boards of the parent entities understand museum ethics and best practices. The Accreditation Commission of the American Alliance of Museums requires that museums operating within a parent organization document the parent organization's commitment to ethical practice, including evidence that it is committed to following AAM and museum field standards, particularly with regard to the museum's collections, the use of deaccessioning proceeds, and collecting and gift-acceptance policies. While not every museum is accredited, this standard represents best practice in the field.[8]

Some museum bylaws specify two layers of governance: the actual governing board and a larger group, often called "overseers" or "the corporation." These bodies are often strictly honorary or ceremonial, although some take a more active role in supporting the museum. The Governance Committee may have responsibility, under the bylaws, for nominating or recommending members to this group as well.

Another factor that can result in multiple boards is when there is a foundation created to provide financial support to the museum. This is most common in university or public museums, but it may also arise when the founding documents of the museum dictate a very small board or one with limited representation (such as the fiduciaries of the donor's trust). It is good practice to have some shared membership between the museum board and the foundation board to ensure regular, open communication.

Groups that are organized to provide advice and support outside of the governing board are also an excellent way to introduce people to the work of the museum. Some boards use advisory councils as a way to cultivate and audition potential board members as well as a way to retain a connection with retired members. Governance experts suggest using a word other than "board" to describe these bodies to avoid confusion about the scope of responsibilities. Advisory councils may be general or organized to involve a particular constituency, such as artists, teachers, or neighbors. Like any ad hoc committee, advisory groups should have a clear scope of role and responsibilities.

MORE PRODUCTIVE MEETINGS

Meeting attendance is lower for museum boards than other types of nonprofits. Of those who responded to the *Museum Board Leadership 2017* survey, only 25 percent reported 90–100 percent attendance, while 21 percent reported just 50–74 percent.[9] In order to build attendance, it is essential to maximize the productivity of board meetings so members feel their time is being put to good use. The trend is definitely toward less time spent on routine matters and reporting in order to leave more time for deliberative discussion and board education. There is also a trend toward less frequent board meetings. Here are some general principles to follow in order to make board meetings more efficient and effective:

- Send out agendas and preparatory materials well in advance.
- Begin and end meetings on time to show respect for members.
- Introduce and welcome all newcomers and guests.

- Start, don't end, with the most strategic issues.
- Make sure every member has an opportunity to speak—especially the quiet ones.
- Encourage members to ask the hard questions and engage in dialogue rather than discussion so they can learn more about perspectives other than their own.
- Include time for educating the board both on what is happening at the museum and on issues and trends that have an impact on the profession at large.
- Poll the board about the frequency, time, length, and location of board meetings to find those that are most convenient, particularly as the board becomes more diverse.

Respondents to the *Museum Board Leadership 2017* survey reported that 45 percent of time in board meetings is spent on routine reports and 23 percent on fiduciary issues, leaving less than a third of their time to focus on strategic issues.[10] Board meetings are best used for governing and looking forward, not backward. That's why more and more boards are using a consent agenda to free board members' time for the essential functions of governing: thinking together about the museum's mission and strategic direction and making decisions that impact its future. A consent agenda is "a bundle of items that is voted on, without discussion, as a package. It differentiates between routine matters not needing explanation and more complex issues needing examination."[11] After approving a motion to adopt the consent agenda format for board meetings, the Governance Committee should develop guidelines on what may or may not be included in the consent portion of the agenda. Typical consent agenda items include the following:

- Approval of the minutes of previous meeting
- Director's report
- Reports on staff and committee activities
- Final action on issues that have been discussed in prior meetings
- Informational materials such as reports that do not require board action
- Updated organizational documents
- Routine items requiring board authorization such as letters and contracts

All supporting and informational materials for items on the consent agenda should be sent out well in advance of the meeting with the expectation that members will read them carefully because, unless called for, there will be no further discussion of these items at the meeting.

At the start of the meeting, the presiding officer asks whether anyone would like to request an item be moved from the consent agenda to the full agenda for further discussion. (Asking questions about items on a consent agenda is not an option, so if there are any items that require clarification, this must be requested *before* the meeting.) If an item requires discussion, a request is made for that item to be removed from the consent agenda. There is then a motion, second, and vote to accept the items in the consent agenda.

Use of consent agendas can lead to board meetings that are structured in a way that is stimulating rather than "mind-numbingly boring." Thomas McLaughlin contrasts a typical board agenda with a strategic agenda.[12] The former, which includes routine reports from the director and committee chairs, "obscures any signals about what is important and what is not." A strategic agenda is forward looking rather than backward looking. Instead of compartmentalizing the work of different committees, it links them together, building momentum toward common goals identified in the strategic plan.

The use of both consent agendas and strategic agendas will maximize the considerable resources that exist around the board table, improving board performance, and increasing board satisfaction. When the board's minds and imaginations are engaged in exploration, learning, and dialogue, attendance at board meetings always improves.[13]

USE OF EXECUTIVE SESSION

Increasingly, boards are reserving time at their meetings for executive sessions, which may involve board members only or include the director but no other staff. This is a time when the board can discuss its own operations and performance and deal with confidential matters (including personnel issues). It also allows the director to be more frank and forthcoming about sensitive issues than when other staff members are present. "By the board and for the board, executive sessions enable the board to manage itself. They create an appropriate forum for board members to talk openly about topics that warrant special treatment."[14] Making executive sessions a regular option at the end of each meeting avoids the need to call for exceptional meetings. If the director is not present, the board chair should convey the gist of executive session discussions as soon as possible or invite the director back into the meeting at the end of the executive session to complete the discussion. Please note that states with "sunshine laws" may have statutory limits on executive or closed sessions, particularly in public museums. Each board should check its state and local laws.

NOTES

1. BoardSource, *Museum Board Leadership 2017: A National Report* (Washington, DC: BoardSource, 2017), 19.

2. Ibid., 13.

3. Ibid., 13.

4. Ibid., 5.

5. Tivoni Devor, "The Face of Nonprofit Boards: A Network Problem," *Nonprofit Quarterly*, March 4, 2015.

6. Daryl Fischer, Swarupa Anila, and Porchia Moore, "Coming Together to Address Systemic Racism in Museums," *Curator* 60, no. 1 (2017): 23–31.

7. "A Fresh Look at Diversity and Boards, Part 3, Recruiting for Board Diversity," *Blue Avocado*, accessed July 26, 2017, http://blueavocado.org/content/recruiting-board-diversity-part-3-diversity-series.

8. "AAM Accreditation Commission Policy: Statements of Support from Parent Organizations," American Alliance of Museums, accessed July 26, 2017, http://www.aam-us.org/docs/default-source/continuum/statements-of-support-ac-policy.pdf?sfvrsn=4.

9. BoardSource, *Museum Board Leadership 2017*, 5.

10. Ibid., 29.

11. BoardSource, *The Consent Agenda: A Tool for Improving Governance* (Washington, DC: BoardSource, 2006).

12. Thomas McLaughlin, "The Strategic Board Agenda," *Board Café*, December 23, 2002, accessed July 26, 2017, https://www.compasspoint.org/board-cafe/strategic-board-agenda.

13. Laura Roberts, "So You Have a Consent Agenda . . . Now How Do You Fill a Board Meeting?" *New England Museums Now*, Winter 2015.

14. BoardSource, *Executive Sessions: How to Use Them Regularly and Wisely* (Washington, DC: BoardSource, 2007), 1.

1

Understanding the Nominations Cycle

It could be said that the Governance Committee's work is never done. As soon as the committee finishes orienting a new class of trustees, it must begin planning the steps involved in identifying and recruiting the next year's class. There are so many critical tasks in the board-building cycle that it can be overwhelming if postponed until the last few months of the year. In addition, the Governance Committee must be prepared to fill unanticipated vacancies that can occur at any time. It must also have a mechanism for keeping track of unanticipated meetings with potential board prospects and leads on potential board members that come up outside of the annual cycle.

Template 1: Nominations Timeline (figures 1.1–1.4) is a tool the Governance Committee can use to plan and monitor its progress throughout the year. This will help the committee, board, and staff members to generate and sustain the momentum they need. Focusing on the museum's mission and strategic plan will help the committee to stay the course at each stage of the board-building process.

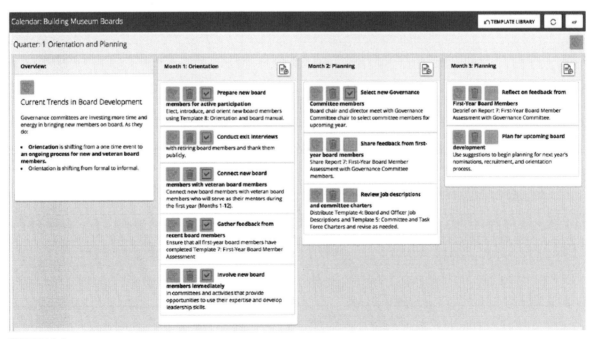

FIGURE 1.1
Nominations Timeline: Quarter 1 (Courtesy of the Museum Trustee Association)

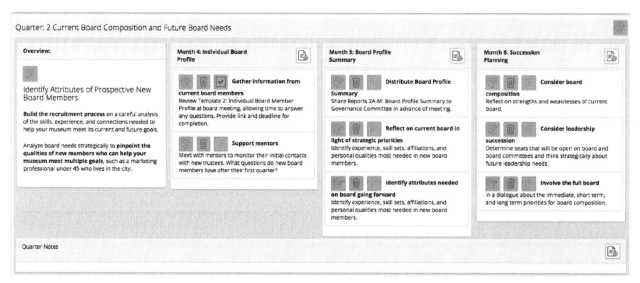

FIGURE 1.2
Nominations Timeline: Quarter 2 (Courtesy of the Museum Trustee Association)

This template provides an overview of the Governance Committee's work in identifying, recruiting, nominating, and orienting new board members. Figures 1.1–1.4 show the yearlong process broken down month by month into quarters. In the sample template, the annual meeting—presumably the date new members are elected to the board—has been fixed in January. The online Help function explains how to adjust the calendar to the start of the board-building cycle in your museum. Since all eight *Building Museum Boards* templates are useful at different stages of the process, references to other templates appear throughout the Nominations Timeline.

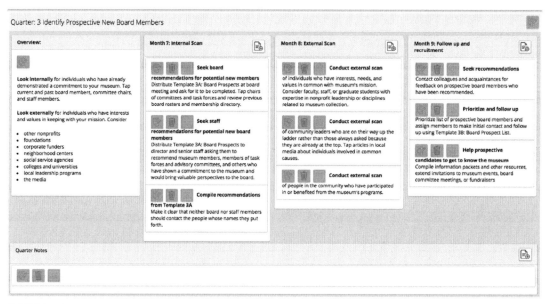

FIGURE 1.3
Nominations Timeline: Quarter 3 (Courtesy of the Museum Trustee Association)

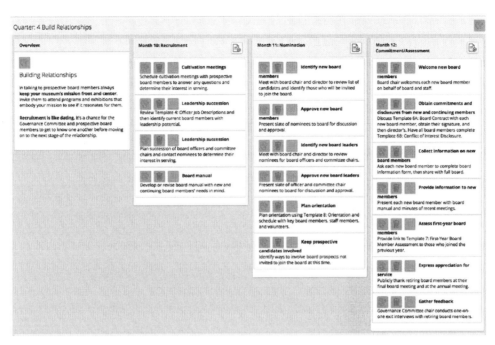

FIGURE 1.4
Nominations Timeline: Quarter 4 (Courtesy of the Museum Trustee Association)

Most activities in a given month focus on a specific step of the board-building process, such as recruitment, nominations, or orientation. Some tasks extend across several months. You can check off each task as it is completed.

- *Month 1*: Elect, introduce, and orient new board members, preparing them for active participation (**Template 8: Orientation**). Distribute **Template 4: Board and Officer Job Descriptions**. Distribute **Template 5: Committee and Task Force Charters** for review and revision by those bodies. Ask board chair to conduct exit / thank you interviews with retiring board members.
- *Month 2*: Compile **Report 7: First-Year Board Member Assessments** from the previous class of board members and form next year's Governance Committee.
- *Month 3*: Review **First-Year Board Member Assessments**, discuss recommendations, and begin to plan next year's board-building process.
- *Month 4*: Gather data from all current board members using **Template 2: Individual Board Member Profile**.
- *Month 5*: Compile individual responses in **Report 2: Board Profile Summary** and **Reports 2A–2M**, and identify experience, skills, and qualities needed on the board.
- *Month 6*: Begin to consider board composition and leadership succession.
- *Month 7*: Conduct an internal scan of individuals who have shown a commitment to the museum, using **Template 3: Board Prospects**.
- *Month 8*: Conduct an external scan of individuals who have interests, needs, and values in common with your mission.
- *Month 9*: Plan and coordinate recruitment efforts using **Template 3: Board Prospects**. Make initial contacts, sharing information about the museum with prospective board members.

- *Month 10*: Continue to cultivate prospective board members and plan leadership succession, referring to **Template 4: Board and Officer Job Descriptions**. Coordinate with the board chair to contact all board members eligible for renewal to determine their interest in and availability to continue serving on the board.
- *Month 11*: Select final candidates with input from the board chair and the director and present slate for board approval.
- *Month 12*: Obtain commitments and disclosures from all board members using **Template 6: Board Contract and Conflict of Interest Disclosure Form**. Gather feedback from first-year board members using **Template 7: First-Year Board Member Assessment**.

When viewed as a whole, these activities represent a comprehensive list of steps to guide board building. Realize that the Governance Committee does not have to complete every step in order to do a good job. Think of this calendar as a checklist of activities to consider rather than a list of tasks that absolutely must be accomplished. Each committee should tailor the process to its own resources and schedule. If your board always takes July and August off, for example, shift events that would fall in those months to June and September.

Take Note!
- Unless otherwise indicated, the Governance Committee performs the tasks and activities on this timeline.
- Some activities, such as partnering new trustees with mentors, extend throughout several months. Be sure to monitor the progress of these activities periodically.
- Cross-references to other templates in *Building Museum Boards* are highlighted throughout Template 1.

2

Gathering Feedback from Current Board Members

Template 2: Individual Board Member Profile is the foundation for board recruitment and nominations. Used to generate the **Board Profile Summary** (Report 2), it helps the Governance Committee identify the expertise, skills, demographic qualities, and personality styles needed to balance the board. This simple form, which takes no more than ten minutes to complete, is an investment that will pay big dividends for the board's future. The online template will ask a series of questions of all board members: basic demographic information, details of their skills and experience, the various ways they contribute to the museum, and their personality styles.

FULL PARTICIPATION COUNTS

Every board member should complete this profile annually, so it should be on the agenda for a board meeting early in the year—perhaps in the second quarter (see **Template 1: Nominations Timeline**). Since this is the first online template, walk everyone through the process of accessing your secure site and opening the Individual Board Profile. Allow time to review the survey together and answer any questions. Since the survey asks respondents to describe themselves, it's important that everyone has the same understanding of the questions posed. Provide a link to your *Templates for Trustees* website and ask everyone to complete the form online by a specific date. Be sure to email the link to trustees who do not attend the meeting with instructions on how to open and complete the survey and the date responses are needed.

CUSTOMIZING THE TEMPLATE

You may customize the template to suit your museum's needs by changing some of the response options listed in certain categories. The Governance Committee should review all of the questions and answers and adjust them to fit the museum's particular circumstances. For example:

- Under Geographic Location, you will need to modify the generic descriptions ("town one," "town two") to fit your museum's service area. If your board has members from outside of its immediate area, the "regional" and "national" categories may apply.
- If your museum is in a community or region with specific ethnic populations not reflected in the options for Ethnic Background, such as Native Alaskan or Native Hawaiian, customize the choices to reflect those. To accurately reflect the particular makeup of your community or region, you may also want to include smaller, more specific places of origin such as Haitian American, Japanese American, or Southeast Asian American.
- The Governance Committee should review the long lists of experience, skills, and areas of influence and select the most relevant choices.

- The dollar ranges under giving and raising funds should be adjusted to reflect the resources of your particular museum and community.

Once the appropriate options have been identified, the administrator can revise the online survey and send an email with a link to each board member, including a reminder to complete it by a specified date. As each member responds, the data is entered into the application. Because the Governance Committee needs to understand what each board member brings to the table, these responses are not confidential. However, they can be seen only by the Governance Committee, not the full board.

If a member is unable to complete the survey online, the administrator can download the Word file in the Museum Documents folder, customize it to match the online survey, print and mail it, and then input the responses. The online Help function explains how to enter surveys. However, we suggest that option be offered only when necessary.

WHY DOES PERSONALITY MATTER?

At the Museum Trustee Association's Assembly 2001: Museum Governance in a New Age, Harvard University professor and governance expert Richard Chait observed that more boards falter from bad chemistry and poor group dynamics than from lack of expertise. He recommends that boards seek a balance of personal traits as well as professional experience and knowledge when recruiting members. The six categories at the end of this profile are not a definitive inventory of personality styles. They do, however, suggest qualities that can impact one-on-one and group communication.

Brian O'Connell believes that it is every bit as important to look for complementary human qualities as it is to look for specific skills or experience. More than ten years ago, he made an observation that still applies. In *The Board Member's Book*, he lamented that often "the only points relate to specific skills and representations and pay no regard to the human qualities that in the end will make the difference in whether it's a board or a barrel of tigers."[1]

While a balance of personality styles is always important, there are stages of the institutional life cycle when certain traits may be more needed on the board. For example, young boards involved in startup situations are likely to have a majority of hands-on members who are task oriented, while older boards in well-established museums may have more members who are process oriented.

Take Note!

- Remind trustees to check all responses that apply, unless instructed otherwise.
- In the Financial Contributions and Volunteer Service Contributions sections, responses should apply to your museum only.
- In the Personality Styles section, trustees are asked to check one description in each pair. If they ask, "What if I don't know which one to check?" or "What if both apply to me?" tell them to choose the one option that seems most fitting without overanalyzing their answers. Usually the first response is the best.

A BALANCED BOARD

One of the Governance Committee's most important challenges is to seek balance in each area measured in this profile. The same laws of equilibrium that apply to individuals apply to organizations: it is far easier to move forward and to maintain positive momentum from a position of balance. That's why it is vitally important for organizations that serve the public to have differing views represented on their boards. The collective strengths and resources of a balanced board will contribute not only to the board's effectiveness but also to the health and well-being of the museum and the community it serves.

The needs of the board vary with the size of the organization and where it is in its life cycle. Smaller or younger museums with limited staff may rely on board members to augment staff expertise in areas such as marketing or investment management. Organizations undergoing expansion or change may need board members with special skills required for the transition, such as construction management or new business development. Often, board members provide expertise in emerging fields, such as technology, that the museum has not yet built into its staffing structure.

Whatever the size of the board or the age of the museum, boards and board committees need both tradition bearers who will help the museum remain faithful to its mission and innovators who will propel it toward the future. Like a family, a healthy board will have members of different ages and experience levels.

There are many ways to explore the data gathered from individual board members. Looking at different factors by board class, for example, will show trends in the way your board is growing—trends you may wish to continue or reverse. (Throughout, "board class" refers to the group of board members whose current terms expire in the same year.) You will be able to see and graph the distribution of the entire board and by board class as it relates to the following:

- Age spread
- Gender mix
- Family status
- Ethnic background
- Geographic location
- Expertise
- Skills
- Areas of influence
- Volunteer/community experience
- Financial contributions
- Fundraising
- Volunteer hours
- Personality styles

Every board may not be equally interested in all of the above dimensions. In addition to the sample reports discussed here, the website includes others from which you can choose. Use whichever are most relevant, depending upon your museum's mission, history, resources, and strategic priorities. And remember that you're not just looking for skill sets, like accounting or marketing, but for people who have the knowledge, experience, and perspective—as well as the time and energy—to meet specific needs of your museum at this moment in time. Taking marketing as an example, do you most need someone with experience in print media or social media? In short, focus on what prospective board members can *do* rather than on who they are or what their resume says.

Report 2: Board Profile Summary

Report 2 is a spreadsheet that automatically tabulates the data provided by individual board members in Template 2. These data can be presented in a variety of easily understandable formats: **Reports 2A–2M**. The graphs generated from this spreadsheet provide an overview of the board's composition from multiple perspectives. Aspects of board composition that may have been overlooked will be strikingly clear, and areas that are out of balance will practically beg to be adjusted.

In addition to looking at the board as a whole, each report can be further broken down by board class.

Once each board member's responses are entered, the charts will be built, revealing the characteristics of your board. Each time data are updated—for example, when a new member joins the board—the charts will change accordingly. It is good practice to ask all members to update their forms annually to capture any changes, such as work experience. When an individual leaves the board, their data should be deleted. With these regular updates, the information and the reports remain current.

A Hypothetical Board

Before the data flows from Template 2 to Report 2, all the graphs will be empty. To illustrate what the completed graphs will look like, we have entered data for a hypothetical board. This board has twelve members who serve three-year terms with a limit of two terms. The following selected charts and graphs suggest what needs the Governance Committee might identify for new board members.

- Board Profile (Report 2, figure 2.1). Because this is a comparatively small board, it is easy to scan the summary report for basic information. Keeping track of who is in which board class and whether they can be nominated for additional term(s) is key to managing the composition of the board and planning the work of the Governance Committee. There is just one member in the class of 2018 who is not eligible for reelection. If the membership of the board is fixed at twelve members, the Governance Committee may have only one open seat to fill. However, it cannot be assumed that the other three members will stand for reelection. The Governance Committee will need to talk with each of them to determine their interest in continuing to serve. Looking ahead, there are two members who are not eligible for reelection in 2019, so the Governance Committee should look ahead and think about prospective members for that year. As you identify areas of concern, you may want to highlight those items on the spreadsheet version of Report 2.
- Age spread of entire board (Report 2A: Age—Full Board, figure 2.2). Almost half of this board is between the ages of fifty-one and sixty-five, 25 percent are over sixty-five, and 25 percent are between thirty-five and fifty. Only one of the members is under thirty-five. While this board is more balanced than many, seeking additional members under thirty-five would bring the perspectives of younger audiences to the board table.
- Ethnic background by board class (Report 2D: Ethnic Background—By Class, figure 2.3). Members of the class of 2018 include three White/Euro Americans and one Asian/Pacific Island American. The class of 2019 has three White/Euro Americans, one Hispanic/Latino American, and one African American member. The class of 2020 has two African Americans, one American Indian/Native American, and one White/Euro American member, perhaps reflecting a greater emphasis on diversity in recent nominating cycles. (Because respondents can check more than one ethnicity, there may be more than twelve answers.) Depending on the ethnic makeup of your community, recruiting an Arab American board member and additional Asian/Pacific Island American, Hispanic/Latino American, or American Indian/Native American members may be a priority.
- Expertise of entire board (Report 2F: Expertise—Full Board, figure 2.4). This board has four members with experience in the corporate sector. Technology, law, and education are also well represented with three members each. The board is light on experience in financial management/investments and accounting, relying on just one member with those areas of expertise (which is revealed in Report 2). Moreover, there is no board experience in marketing, public relations, visitor studies, or programs/special events. With audience development a key part of many museums' strategic plans, the Governance Committee should seek experience in these areas in the next class of board members. (Since many people bring expertise in more than one area, like a lawyer who has experience in property management, the number of bars will exceed the number of people on the board.)

Report 2: Individual Board Member Profile		Abigail Allen, Class: 2018, Eligible: False	Bob Burns, Class: 2020, Eligible: True	Carol Cohen, Class: 2020, Eligible: True	Danetta Davis, Class: 2020, Eligible: True	Edward Evans, Class: 2019, Eligible: False	Frank Fitzgerald, Class: 2018, Eligible: True	Grace Gordon, Class: 2018, Eligible: True	Harold Humphries, Class: 2019, Eligible: False	Ingrid Ireland, Class: 2019, Eligible: True	Julio Jimenez, Class: 2019, Eligible: True	Ken Kraft, Class: 2020, Eligible: True	Lee Liu, Class: 2018, Eligible: True	Total
A: Age	Under 35		1											1
	35-50					1					1	1		3
	51-65	1		1				1	1	1				5
	Over 65				1		1						1	3
A: Age Total		1	1	1	1	1	1	1	1	1	1	1	1	12
B: Gender	Female	1		1	1			1		1			1	6
	Male		1			1	1		1		1	1		6
B: Gender Total		1	1	1	1	1	1	1	1	1	1	1	1	12
C: Family Status	No Children		1	1										2
	With Preschool Children					1								1
	With School Age Children											1		1
	With Teenage Children								1	1	1			3
	With Grown Children				1		1						1	3
	Prefer not to answer	1						1						2
C: Family Status Total		1	1	1	1	1	1	1	1	1	1	1	1	12
D: Ethnic Background	Asian/Pacific Island American												1	1
	Black/African American				1						1	1		3
	Hispanic/Latino American										1			1
	American Indian/Native American		1											1
	White/Euro-American	1		1		1	1	1	1	1				7
D: Ethnic Background Total		1	1	1	1	1	1	1	1	1	2	1	1	13
E: Geographic Location	City center	1	1	1										3
	Town one				1	1		1						3
	Town two						1		1	1				3
	Town three										1	1		2
	Regional												1	1
E: Geographic Location Total		1	1	1	1	1	1	1	1	1	1	1	1	12
F: Expertise	Accounting				1									1
	Architecture/Landscape						1				1			2
	Business/Corporate				1	1					1	1		4
	Collections									1	1			2
	Communications/Social Media		1								1			2
	Education/Child Development			1					1				1	3
	Financial Mgmt / Investments					1								1
	Fund Raising						1	1						2
	Health Care								1		1			2
	Human Resources				1			1					1	3

FIGURE 2.1

Board Profile Summary: Spreadsheet (Courtesy of the Museum Trustee Association)

Report 2: Individual Board Member Profile		Abigail Allen, Class: 2018, Eligible: False	Bob Burns, Class: 2020, Eligible: True	Carol Cohen, Class: 2020, Eligible: True	Danetta Davis, Class: 2020, Eligible: True	Edward Evans, Class: 2019, Eligible: False	Frank Fitzgerald, Class: 2018, Eligible: True	Grace Gordon, Class: 2018, Eligible: True	Harold Humphries, Class: 2019, Eligible: False	Ingrid Ireland, Class: 2019, Eligible: True	Julio Jimenez, Class: 2019, Eligible: True	Ken Kraft, Class: 2020, Eligible: True	Lee Liu, Class: 2018, Eligible: True	Total
	Law	1					1		1					3
	Nonprofits		1				1	1						3
	Property Management	1												1
	Real Estate					1				1				2
	Social Services			1								1		2
	Technology		1			1					1			3
F: Expertise Total		2	3	2	4	5	3	4	3	4	2	2	2	36
	Mediation			1			1	1					1	4
	Project Management	1	1							1				3
	Strategic Planning				1						1			2
G: Skills	Negotiations	1					1			1			1	4
	Team Building		1			1					1			3
	Community Action			1								1		2
	Advocacy					1		1						2
G: Skills Total		2	2	2	2	1	2	2	2	1	1	1	2	20
	Political	1			1			1						3
	Small Business		1	1										2
	Government		1											1
	Media										1	1		2
H: Areas of Influence	Education			1				1						2
	Religious									1				1
	Tourism					1							1	2
	Corporate										1			1
	Neighborhood					1		1						2
H: Areas of Influence Total		1	1	2	2	2	1	2	1	1	1	1	1	16
	Other Nonprofit Boards		1				1	1						3
	Corporate Boards			1	1						1	1		4
I: Volunteer/ Community Experience	Community Service			1								1		2
	Education/Youth Activities			1				1					1	3
	Religious Organizations									1			1	2
	Arts/Culture	1									1			2
I: Volunteer/ Community Experience Total		1	1	2	1	1	1	2	1	1	1	2	2	16
	$500 - $999		1				1							2
J: Financial Contributions to Museum - Giving	$1000-$4999			1	1			1			1	1	1	6
	$5000-$9999					1				1	1			3
	Greater than $10,000	1												1
J: Financial Contributions to Museum - Giving Total		1	1	1	1	1	1	1	1	1	1	1	1	12
	Less than $500		1				1			1		1		4

FIGURE 2.1
(continued)

Report 2: Individual Board Member Profile		Abigail Allen, Class: 2018, Eligible: False	Bob Burns, Class: 2020, Eligible: True	Carol Cohen, Class: 2020, Eligible: True	Danetta Davis, Class: 2020, Eligible: True	Edward Evans, Class: 2019, Eligible: False	Frank Fitzgerald, Class: 2018, Eligible: True	Grace Gordon, Class: 2018, Eligible: True	Harold Humphries, Class: 2019, Eligible: False	Ingrid Ireland, Class: 2019, Eligible: True	Julio Jimenez, Class: 2019, Eligible: True	Ken Kraft, Class: 2020, Eligible: True	Lee Liu, Class: 2018, Eligible: True	Total
K: Financial Contributions to Museum - Raised	$500 - $999			1		1		1			1			4
	$1000-$4999								1				1	2
	$5000-$9999				1									1
	Greater than $10,000	1												1
K: Financial Contributions to Museum - Raised Total		1	1	1	1	1	1	1	1	1	1	1	1	12
L: Volunteer Service Contributions to Museum	Less than 2 hours/month	1												1
	2 to 5 hours/month			1					1	1	1			4
	6 to 10 hours/month				1			1				1		3
	11 to 20 hours/month					1	1						1	3
	Greater than 20 hours/month		1											1
L: Volunteer Service Contributions to Museum Total		1	1	1	1	1	1	1	1	1	1	1	1	12
M: Personality Styles	Listener	1	1			1	1	1	1	1	1	1		9
	Speaker			1	1								1	3
	Creative, Imaginative	1	1	1			1	1	1	1				7
	Practical, Realistic				1	1			1			1	1	5
	Consensus Builder		1	1			1	1	1	1		1		7
	Devil's Advocate	1			1	1	1				1			5
	Process Oriented	1		1	1			1			1			5
	Task Oriented		1			1	1	1	1	1	1			7
	Innovator		1	1	1							1	1	5
	Traditionalist	1				1	1	1			1	1	1	7
	Convergent Thinker		1		1	1				1	1		1	6
	Divergent Thinker	1		1					1	1		1	1	6
M: Personality Styles Total		6	6	6	6	6	6	6	6	6	6	6	6	72

- Skills of entire board (Report 2G: Skills—Full Board, figure 2.5). The board has only two members with strategic-planning skills. If the museum anticipates engaging in planning in the near future, the Governance Committee should look for members who can bring that expertise to the board.
- Financial contributions and fundraising by board class (Report 2J: Giving—By Class, figure 2.6; and Report 2K: Raised—By Class, figure 2.7). In general, trustees are personally generous but not particularly successful at raising funds. The Governance Committee might work with the Development Committee to improve the board's capacity to cultivate donors and support fundraising. The only trustee who "gives" and "gets" more than $10,000 will retire in 2018, so the Governance Committee will need to look for additional major donors for the board. (You can determine who the generous member is in Report 2.) Why is only one member giving more than

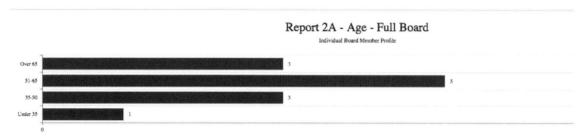

FIGURE 2.2
Board Profile Summary: Age Spread (Courtesy of the Museum Trustee Association)

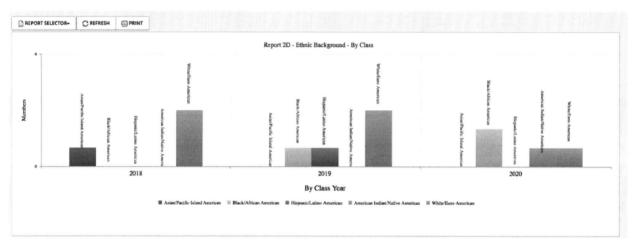

FIGURE 2.3
Board Profile Summary: Ethnic Background (Courtesy of the Museum Trustee Association)

FIGURE 2.4
Board Profile Summary: Expertise (Courtesy of the Museum Trustee Association)

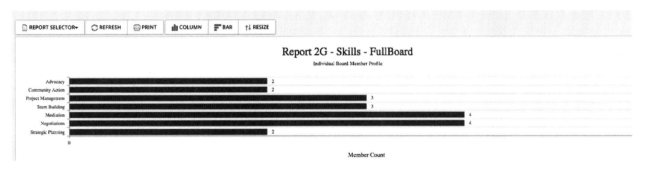

FIGURE 2.5
Board Profile Summary: Skills (Courtesy of the Museum Trustee Association)

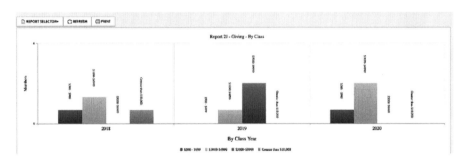

FIGURE 2.6
Board Profile Summary: Financial Contributions (Courtesy of the Museum Trustee Association)

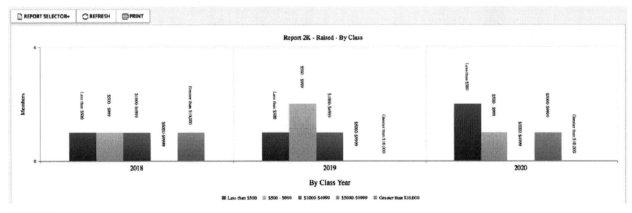

FIGURE 2.7
Board Profile Summary: Fundraising (Courtesy of the Museum Trustee Association)

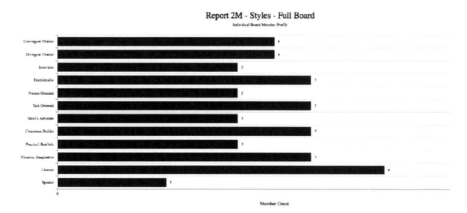

Report 2M - Styles - Full Board

FIGURE 2.8
Board Profile Summary: Personality Styles (Courtesy of the Museum Trustee Association)

$10,000? If gifts in that range are a goal, has it been communicated to board members? Has board recruitment been sufficiently mindful of potential members' philanthropic capacity? Or is that an unrealistic expectation for this museum and this community?

- Personality styles of entire board (Report 2M: Style—Full Board, figure 2.8). There is fairly even distribution between each pair of personality styles, with the exception of Speakers and Listeners. With so many more Listeners than Speakers, the Governance Committee would do well to seek new members who are comfortable speaking out.

NOTE

1. Brian O'Connell, *The Board Member's Book* (New York: The Foundation Center, 2003), 70.

3

Identifying New Board Prospects

Board recruitment is an ongoing team effort, not a one-time event or an individual encounter. **Template 3: Board Prospects** helps those who identify, contact, and recruit board candidates coordinate their efforts and monitor their progress. It creates a database that records and tracks prospective board members, starting with recommendation by a board or staff member, and going through the cultivation and nomination process. The administrator creates a separate record for each prospect and invites members of the board or the executive director to complete Part A, which records basic information about the candidate (figure 3.1 is a sample for a hypothetical candidate). The form can also be shared in hard copy, with information collected and entered by the administrator.

Those who make the referral complete Part A of the template, and those who make the contact(s) complete Part B with regular updates as the cultivation process unfolds. It's worth noting that those making referrals do not necessarily contact the people they recommend. After reviewing the referrals gathered from Part A, the chair of the Governance Committee will ask specific committee members to follow up with those prospects that will be pursued. They will complete the appropriate sections of Part B. In some cases, it may be helpful to create two tiers of prospects so recruiters can start with those individuals who have the skill sets and experience most needed in new board members and move on to the second tier if necessary.

RECOMMENDING PROSPECTS

Part A provides a variety of information that will help the Governance Committee decide whether to move ahead with the recruitment process for an individual who has been recommended. Print the Word document of the form (in Museum Documents folder) and distribute copies at the board meeting when you discuss the current board profile and prioritize the needs for future board members (see **Template 1: Nominations Timeline**). You may also want to set aside time at a staff meeting to solicit ideas. All board members and the executive director are able to create and edit prospective board member profiles on the website. You may also offer the option of circulating the form, either in hard copy or electronically, asking members to submit the form to the Governance Committee and having the administrator enter the information. In this age of social media, the Governance Committee might also elect to look at candidates' online accounts and profiles to get a sense of their interests, activities, and priorities.

TRACKING THE RECRUITMENT PROCESS

Recruiting a new board member is rarely accomplished in a single meeting or even a single year. The cultivation of a new board member, especially in the case of someone unfamiliar with the museum, should not be rushed. Time invested in getting to know prospective board members and letting them get to know the museum will pay big dividends. The recruitment process is a lot like dating. Whether the relationship begins as a blind date or as

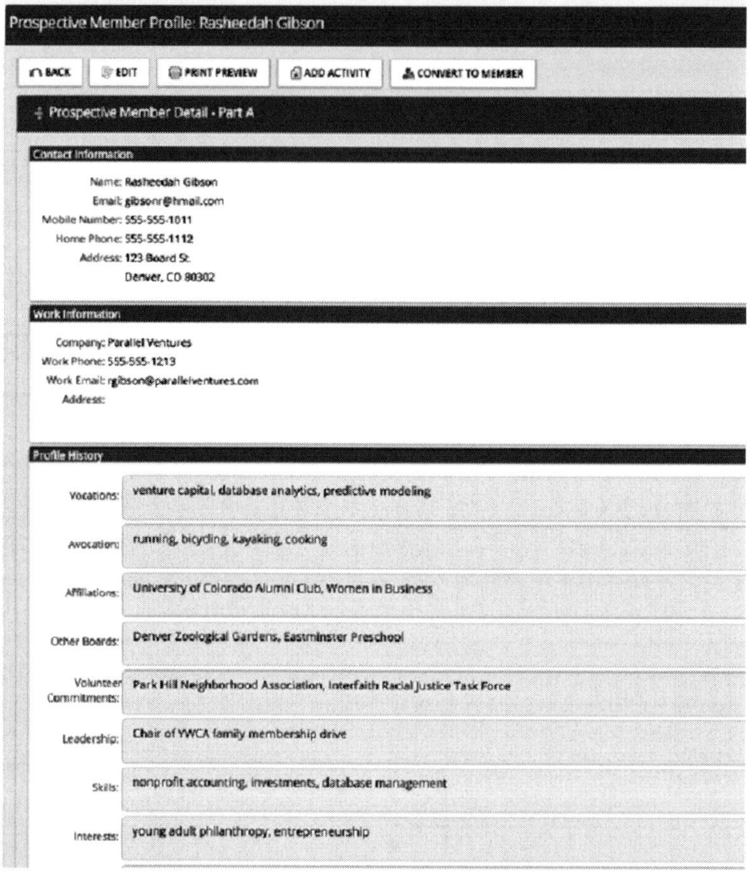

FIGURE 3.1
Prospective Board Member Profile: Part A
(Courtesy of the Museum Trustee Association)

a meeting of old friends, it has to progress through various stages. Once the contact person and the prospective board member have met, they need to determine whether there is a mutual interest in continuing the relationship. If so, they will arrange opportunities to get to know each other better—to "meet the family," so to speak, through invitations to exhibitions, special events, fundraisers, or board meetings.

After the Governance Committee reviews all of the prospective members and decides who should move onto the stage of cultivation, a member of the committee is given responsibility for coordinating the cultivation process and recording all of the connections between the museum and the prospective member in Part B. As candidates are approached, the outcomes of initial and subsequent meetings are recorded in the prospect's record. The contact person can record phone calls, text messages, emails, meetings, attendance at programs or events, or invitations to board or committee meetings, as well as questions that the prospective board member asks. After each meeting, the contact person can make brief notes about how the relationship is developing. (Figure 3.2 continues the process for the hypothetical candidate.) The steps in Part B provide a checklist for the stages in the recruitment and cultivation process. Not all of them are necessary, but certain steps—the initial contact, the cultivation meeting, the invitation, and the recommendation to the board—are especially important.

Once all of the candidates have been approached and cultivated, the Governance Committee will meet to identify those who will make the best additions to the board as a whole. This requires striking a balance between the assets of each prospective board member and the needs of the current board, giving special consideration to those who are, or will soon be, leaving the board. Here it will be helpful to review **Report 2A: Board Profile Summary**.

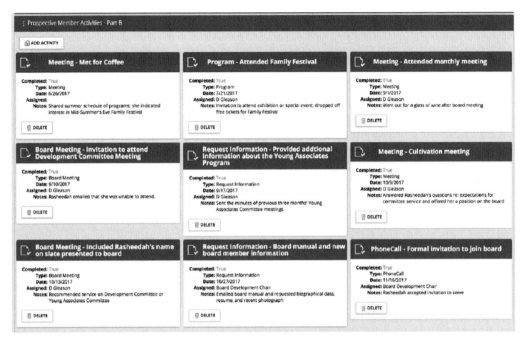

FIGURE 3.2
Prospective Board Member Activities: Part B (Courtesy of the Museum Trustee Association)

After coming to consensus, the committee will be in a position to present the slate in accordance with the bylaws. Typically the full board is asked to take an up or down vote on the entire slate, not to vote on individual members.

Those who are invited to join the board and accept the invitation are changed to "board member" role and all the information gathered becomes part of their board profile. Those who defer nomination and those who the committee would like to keep under consideration are retained in the application and the full record will be available to next year's Governance Committee. Those who are dropped from consideration can simply be deleted.

Take Note!
- This template is marked "confidential" to respect the privacy of prospective board members who may or may not be invited to join the board. It should be shared only with members of the Governance Committee and the contact person(s) for each prospective board member.
- Forms can be retained from year to year, so if a strong prospect defers until a future cycle, information about that potential board member and all of the contacts are available for the next year's nominating process.
- Be sure to emphasize to those making referrals that they *must not contact* the individuals they recommend until and unless asked to do so by the Governance Committee.

4

Clarifying Board Roles

Template 4: Board and Officer Job Descriptions includes a document with typical responsibilities for board officers and members at large. It may be particularly helpful to newly established boards or new board leaders who aren't sure where to assign responsibilities.

Some tasks are clearly the responsibility of one officer or another. The chair presides at meetings; the treasurer oversees the financial affairs of the museum. But other tasks vary, depending upon the traditions of the institution, the interests and skills of individuals on the board, and specific needs at any given time. For example, a chair who usually develops agendas for board meetings may assign this task to the vice chair, leaving the chair with more time to devote to a capital campaign or other special project. These job descriptions are guidelines, not prescriptions. The goals and needs of your museum should determine the actual responsibilities of board officers, committees, and task forces.

To tailor the job descriptions to your own board, a member of the Governance Committee, working with the board chair and the director, should edit the bulleted lists, adding or deleting responsibilities or moving them from one board position to another. The museum's bylaws should be a starting point for the officers and their mandated tasks and responsibilities, but most officers have other duties as well. The list of "duties that may be assigned to any officer or member of the board" is a starting point for further customization. Your board may have additional officers (chair, chair-elect, first vice chair, assistant secretary, assistant treasurer, for example), requiring additional job descriptions.

Tasks with an asterisk may not be applicable to all boards, so eliminate any that are not relevant to yours. For example, if there is no functioning Executive Committee, all of those references should be deleted.

As the administrator creates a job description for each member, he or she can delete information that is not relevant to that member's role on the board.

Take Note!

- There is no question that board members and directors want a constructive relationship; however, there can be inherent tensions in the working relationship. Because the executive director reports to the board, this can create an ambiguous situation when board members or board committees fulfill operational tasks as volunteers, something that is more likely to happen in small and emerging museums. In these cases, it will help for board members to keep in mind whether they're seated around the board table wearing their board hats or helping out at a community event wearing their volunteer hats.

- On some boards, the past chair continues to attend board meetings for a defined period of time. To facilitate the leadership transition, he or she may advise the board and Executive Committee. In consultation with the current chair, the past chair may also undertake a special project that builds on strategic priorities established during his or her term.

TEMPLATE 4: BOARD AND OFFICER JOB DESCRIPTIONS

{[Museum Name]}

{[Mission Statement]}

Instructions: This template includes a list of responsibilities for all board members and four officer job descriptions. To tailor it for each member:

- Customize the list of responsibilities, considering the "duties that may be assigned to any officer or member of the board" at the end of this template
- Add any committee assignments or chair positions
- In particular, note tasks with an asterisk and delete those that are not applicable
- Insert the number of permitted meeting absences in accordance with bylaws or operating policies
- Keep appropriate officer job descriptions, changing the title where needed
- Delete other officer positions

When done, delete these instructions and save the completed document to the member's record.

{[full name]}

Members of the board have the following responsibilities:

- Learn about and remain informed of the {[Museum Name]}'s collections, operations, bylaws, policies, programs, and finances
- Keep current on local, regional, national, and international developments in the museum's field of collecting
- Promote the museum in the community by speaking knowledgeably about its collections, exhibitions, and programs
- Prospect for potential partnerships and collaborations in the community
- Review agenda and supporting materials prior to meetings
- Attend board meetings with no more than [insert number] absences per year*
- Serve on at least one committee and take on special assignments as needed, sharing expertise with staff and fellow trustees or identifying others who can help
- Act in the best interests of the museum, abstaining from discussions and votes that involve a conflict of interest
- Join the museum and pay regular membership dues, increasing level of membership whenever possible
- Encourage friends and business associates to join the museum, helping to identify new members
- Contribute to the museum's financial well-being with a substantial annual contribution
- Seek financial support from others by engaging in solicitation

- Support fundraisers by planning, attending, and/or volunteering
- When volunteering, recognize that board members serve in a support, rather than a governance, capacity
- Serve as spokespersons and ambassadors to the community on behalf of the museum
- Attend exhibitions, programs, and special events
- Identify opportunities for the museum to increase its visibility locally, regionally, and nationally
- Contribute specialized knowledge in areas of expertise/interest when called upon by staff or fellow trustees
- Initiate contacts with other needed sources of outside expertise

The Chair will:
- Represent the board as a whole
- Oversee board affairs
- Serve as primary liaison to the director
- Work with director to ensure compliance with the bylaws
- Work with director to identify best practices that will be used as benchmarks in governance
- Develop agendas for meetings in concert with director
- Preside at board meetings, facilitating constructive dialogue and making sure all views are heard
- Preside at annual meeting
- Foster a unity of purpose that unites individuals with diverse personalities and perspectives
- Preside at Executive Committee meetings*
- Appoint chairs for each committee and task force and maintain ongoing communication
- Serve as an ex officio member of all committees and task forces*
- Represent the museum to the community as the official board voice
- Oversee partnerships/collaborations with other institutions
- Speak to the media, the community, and government agencies or recommend other board members, as appropriate

The Vice Chair will:
- Act as the chair in his or her absence
- Preside at board meetings in the absence of the chair
- Assist chair as needed
- Serve as liaison between committee/task force chairs and Executive Committee*
- Serve on Executive Committee*
- Complete special projects, as assigned by president
- Serve as chair-elect, assuming leadership when current chair retires*

The Treasurer will:

- Facilitate board understanding of financial status and responsibilities
- Ensure that accurate and timely financial reports are presented to [the Executive Committee and*] the full board
- Provide drafts of annual budget for board approval
- Present regular budget reports, answering board questions
- Present special budget reports, explaining unusual situations
- Attend the annual meeting to present annual budget and key financial events and take questions from members
- Serve as chair of Finance Committee*
- Prepare agenda and calendar for Finance Committee meetings*
- With the finance committee, manage and monitor performance of investments*
- Work with accounting staff in developing and implementing financial procedures and systems
- Oversee the timely filing of tax forms and audit process
- Serve on Executive Committee*

The Secretary will:

- Prepare and distribute agendas and information for meetings of the board, [Executive Committee,*] and general membership
- Write and distribute minutes of all meetings
- Ensure that all notices are given in accordance with bylaws
- Draft documents and special reports as needed
- Write and maintain files of official correspondence
- Act as custodian of corporate records
- Serve on Executive Committee*

Duties that may be assigned to any officer or member of the board:

- Recommend committees that need to be established or disbanded, formed, or reformed
- eek volunteers and assist president in coordinating individual board member assignments
- Establish traditions for recognizing and rewarding board service
- Recognize and formally thank retiring board members
- Serve on director Search Committee and articulate goals and job description for position of director*
- Participate in evaluating director and negotiating compensation and benefits package
- Serve as [chair or member] of [Name] Committee*
- Serve as [chair or member] of [Name] Task Force*

Delineating Committees and Task Forces

STANDING COMMITTEES OR TASK FORCES?

Museum Board Leadership 2017 suggests that board committees have pros and cons. On the positive side, they can provide individual board members with opportunities to delve into issues of strategic importance while supporting the work of the full board. On the flip side, they can give the false impression that only those board members who serve on specific committees need to pay attention to issues such as fundraising or finances.[1] To build boards that are responsive and dynamic, board committees must have a clear statement of purpose and be based on institutional strategy rather than on organizational structure. Increasingly, boards are finding that task forces, project teams, work groups, and ad hoc committees function more strategically than "standing committees," which, as pointed out by Richard Chait, are aptly named.[2]

Task forces can be more focused on the board's current priorities and future goals than on its ongoing responsibilities and long-standing traditions. They can also be more agile than standing committees, responding quickly to the requirements of a particular project without having to channel their work through the normal board hierarchy. They can more readily include people with specific expertise or networks appropriate to the task at hand without requiring the long-term commitment of a seat on the board. When a project is completed, the task force disbands, often leaving members with a real sense of accomplishment.

Boards can attract a broader spectrum of participants when people sign on for a specific and finite task rather than an ongoing responsibility. This kind of commitment is often a better fit for two groups: up-and-coming young professionals who have a lot of talent—and many things to juggle in their personal and professional lives—and mature leaders who are asked to do so much by so many. When these individuals come together, they are able to focus their energies on current strategic priorities rather than on board traditions. For non-board members, it's a way to get to know the board's culture and values; for the board, it's a way to audition prospective new members while gaining fresh insights.

Task forces may also be appropriate when the work to be done is more operational than typical board functions can be, such as working with an architect or contractor on a building project or developing a new brand for the museum. Board members and others can extend the capacity of paid staff without upsetting the delicate balance between policy and management.

Though most boards will always have a need for some standing committees, such as Executive, Finance, Audit, Collections, and Governance, it's important to be clear about the purpose and charge of each committee. The Governance Committee may be in the best position to examine standing committees, posing such questions as:

- Does this committee serve a vital, ongoing function?
- What, specifically, does it exist to accomplish?

- Is its scope of responsibility clearly distinguished from staff functions, in order to avoid ambiguity?
- Should its purpose be expanded or redefined?
- Would a task force or ad hoc committee be equally or more effective?

In terms of experience, the charge of some committees may require more experienced members than others, but all committees will benefit from a regular infusion of new perspectives. In terms of size, some committees may require more members than others. The Governance Committee should look for deviations from the norm—the smaller or larger committees—and ask why. Do smaller committees need more members? Are larger committees functioning effectively?

Those who serve on standing committees represent a valuable resource in terms of their time and talents. How can boards make the best use of these assets, keeping standing committees vital, focused, and active, perhaps by applying some of the principles of task forces?

- Meet only when there is important business to conduct. There is nothing sacred about monthly meetings; unnecessary meetings can dilute the urgency and importance of a committee's tasks.
- Be clear about each committee's purpose and try to reflect that purpose in the committee's name. For example, renaming the Building and Grounds Committee the Community Spaces and Services Committee can empower members to consider how properties are used as well as their condition.[3]

Each organization must determine the optimum number and appropriate functions of standing committees and task forces based on its mission, vision, and strategic goals. Any board committee will function more effectively when it is task driven and integrated within the board structure. The Governance Committee must ensure that its charge to each of the committees—standing and ad hoc—is clear and strategic.

TEMPLATE 5: COMMITTEE AND TASK FORCE CHARTERS
This template includes a standard form for creating the charters of standing committees. The charter has five components:

- Purpose
- Responsibilities
- Membership
- Meetings
- Authority

The appendix of this book includes short descriptions of the purposes and responsibilities of six of the most common standing committees (audit, collections, development, executive, finance, and governance) and two ad hoc task forces (strategic planning and annual fundraiser). The Word document is also in the Museum Documents folder in the *Building Museum Boards* online application. The trend in nonprofit governance is to have fewer standing committees and more ad hoc committees responsible for completing a specific project or task, such as strategic planning, capital projects, or a special event. When completing a charter for a task force, note the expected time frame for the project or event under purpose.

To customize the template, open it and insert the committee or task force name. Complete the five sections in turn, referring to the museum's bylaws, board handbook, or board meeting minutes as well as the appendix to find all the relevant information. The incumbent chair of each committee should be involved in the drafting of the

TEMPLATE 5: BOARD COMMITTEE AND TASK FORCE CHARTERS

{[Museum Name]}

{[Mission Statement]}

Standing Committees and Ad Hoc Task Forces

Charter

[Committee or Task Force Name]

Purpose

- General statement of the committee's scope of responsibilities and, where appropriate, reference to the source of its authority, such as bylaws, board resolution, etc.
- If ad hoc committee or task force, projected duration of the project, event, or initiative

Responsibilities

- Enumeration of committee responsibilities beyond the general statement of purpose

Membership

- Details on who serves on the committee: board members, non-board members, ex officio members, members representing affiliated groups, etc.
- Details on any policy or bylaws commitments on number of members

Meetings

- Details on number and/or timing of meetings if set

Authority

- If the committee is empowered (or, in ambiguous situations, NOT empowered) to act for the full board and/or to make commitments on behalf of the museum

charter for their committee. Once tailored to your museum, the charters should be reviewed and adopted by the full board.

Take Note!

- It is good practice for each committee to review its charter annually and update it as appropriate. Committees should also be encouraged to refer to the museum's strategic plan and implementation plan and identify their priorities each year.

- Often bylaws or board policies specify that the board chair is an ex officio member of all committees. To support the succession of board leadership, consider moving some or all of that responsibility to the vice chair or chair elect.
- Succession planning should be carried out at the committee level as well as with the full board. Long-serving committee chairs should be encouraged to identify possible successors and share leadership responsibility.
- If permitted by the museum's bylaws, committees should include non-board members with needed skills, expertise, or connections to the community. Committee work is an excellent way to bring donors, community members, and potential board members closer to the work of the museum.
- Most standing committees and some task forces are doing work delegated by the board. Non-board members serving on those committees and task forces should receive the conflict of interest policy statement and disclosure form (Template 6, Part B) to complete.

NOTES

1. BoardSource, *Museum Board Leadership 2017: A National* Report (Washington, DC: BoardSource, 2017), 14.

2. Richard Chait, "The New Work of the Nonprofit Board," presentation at the American Association of Museums Annual Meeting, Baltimore, Maryland, May 5, 2000.

3. Daryl Fischer, "The Incredible Disappearing Committee," *Board Member* 13, no. 8 (December 2004): 14–15.

6

Securing Commitments from Board Members

Template 6: Board Contract and Conflict of Interest Disclosure Form includes three documents. Part A is an agreement that outlines the mutual responsibilities of board members and museum leadership; Part B is a conflict of interest disclosure statement. There is also a sample conflict of interest policy, which should be customized for each institution.

BOARD CONTRACT

All board members must agree to uphold the standards of trusteeship known as the duty of care, the duty of obedience, and the duty of loyalty. Along with these general principles come specific responsibilities to be a good steward, provide financial support, and provide leadership to the museum.

For the trustee, serving on a museum board is a multifaceted commitment that brings with it responsibilities for stewardship, financial support, and governance. For the museum, working with a board brings responsibilities for orientation, ongoing training, communication, and indemnification. Both parties must meet these mutual responsibilities in order to work as partners for the good of the museum and the community it serves. In signing these documents, both the trustee and the director agree to fulfill their respective responsibilities.

The museum's mission statement appears on the contract to remind each party why they are making these commitments. As the museum's chief executive, the director agrees to give the board member the necessary introductions, orientation, ongoing education, and information needed to carry out his or her responsibilities. The museum also agrees to insure the trustee against liability to the full extent of the law. Indemnification of trustees may be written into the museum's bylaws.

Tailor this contract to your museum, and personalize it to each new board member. We suggest discussing it at a full board meeting and creating a document that captures the museum's expectations, values, and priorities. As currently designed, customization would include the following steps:

- The program will insert the director's name, title, and the museum's name in the first paragraph. The administrator should insert applicable guidelines for notification of meetings and distribution of minutes.
- The program will insert each board member's name.
- In the third section ("To be a good steward, I will . . ."), the administrator will insert the minimum standards for attendance at board meetings, as established by the Governance Committee or in the bylaws.
- In the fourth section ("To provide financial support, I will . . ."), the board member will fill in his or her fundraising and giving commitments, consistent with expectations established by the Governance Committee or board policy. The administrator will customize the list of the museum's fundraisers.

TEMPLATE 6A: BOARD CONTRACT

Greenville Museum of History and Art

Greenville Museum of Art and History broadens and deepens the community's connections to the heritage and culture of the region.

I, Jordan Charles, executive director of the Greenville Museum of History and Art (hereinafter called "the museum"), agree to provide each member of the board with:

- An introduction to other board members and key staff members
- An orientation to the museum, its mission, collection, organizational structure, and culture
- Ongoing education in the form of retreats and other board development opportunities
- Relevant and current information about the operations of the museum
- Access to information about the museum's permanent collection and special exhibitions
- Access to information about best practices in the museum profession and nonprofit governance
- Regular reports of income and expenses that provide useful analysis of relevant financial data
- A list of expectations for board members and an opportunity to clarify any that may be unclear
- Opportunities to discuss the museum's goals, programs, and activities with the director and board president
- Notice of all meetings with agendas and necessary support materials at least [insert length of time as days or weeks] in advance
- Minutes of all board meetings within [insert length of time as days or weeks] of meetings
- Insurance providing indemnification from liability for reasonable and necessary actions of the board to the extent outlined in the bylaws

I, Abigail Allen, agree to serve the Greenville Museum of History and Art to the best of my ability. I support the mission of the museum and understand that I am legally and ethically responsible for carrying out my responsibilities according to the following standards:

- The Duty of Obedience is a standard of trust, which states that a board member will be faithful to the museum's mission and fulfill the public trust by acting in ways that are consistent with the museum's mission.
- The Duty of Care is a standard of competence, which is described as "the care that an ordinarily prudent person would exercise in a similar position under similar circumstances."
- The Duty of Loyalty is a standard of faithfulness, which dictates that a board member will give undivided allegiance to the museum when making decisions that affect it, never using inside information for personal or professional gain.

To be a good steward, I will:

- Subscribe to the museum's mission statement and strategic goals, exercising fair, independent judgment and due care in all decision-making

- Excuse myself from any discussions or votes where I have a conflict of interest
- Subscribe to the museum's code of ethics, disclosing any potential conflicts of interest and putting the good of the museum before personal interests or financial gain
- Learn about and remain informed of the museum's collections, operations, policies, programs, and finances
- Keep current on local, regional, national, and international developments in the museum's field
- Attend board meetings and committee meetings with no more than two absences per year, carefully reviewing agenda and supporting materials prior to meetings
- Serve on at least one committee and take on special assignments as needed, sharing my expertise with staff and fellow trustees or identifying others who can help
- Avoid competing with the museum for the acquisition of objects it wishes to add to its collection

To provide financial support, I will:
- Join the museum and pay regular membership dues, increasing my level of membership whenever possible
- Encourage friends and business associates to join the museum, helping to identify ___ new members per year
- Include the museum among my highest philanthropic priorities and contribute to its financial well-being with a substantial annual contribution; I pledge to give at least $_____ monthly/quarterly/annually (circle one); I reserve the right to modify this commitment in the event of unforeseen circumstances
- Seek financial support from others by engaging in solicitation to individuals and groups in my circle of acquaintances; I will aim to raise $_____ annually
- Support the following fundraisers by planning, attending, and/or volunteering
  - [Fundraiser name]
  - [Fundraiser name]
  - [Fundraiser name]
  - [Fundraiser name]

To provide leadership, I will:
- Serve as a spokesperson and ambassador to the community on behalf of the museum
- Attend exhibitions and programs in order to have a visible role and experience the museum from the perspective of its visitors
- Identify opportunities for the museum to increase its visibility, locally, regionally, and nationally
- Maintain confidentiality on issues discussed at board and committee meetings
- Contribute specialized knowledge in my areas of expertise/interest when called upon by staff or fellow trustees
- Initiate contacts with other needed sources of outside expertise
- Understand the distinct but complementary roles of board and staff, respecting the expertise and authority of the director

This contract shall be renewable annually, at the time of the museum's annual meeting.

Signed and dated:

Abigail Allen, Board Member

Jordan Charles, Executive Director

Once the contract is complete, it should be printed in two hard copies to be completed by the board member and signed by the board member and the director. The administrator then gives the board member a signed copy and retains one for the board files.

Both the individual board member and the director of the museum should review the contract carefully before signing it. New board members should be given a copy of the contract when they accept the board's nomination and invited to ask questions about the commitment they are making. Although this contract is not a legal document, it establishes mutual expectations for performance and sets the stage for a standard of clear written communication between the museum and the board.

CONFLICT OF INTEREST POLICY AND DISCLOSURE STATEMENT

The IRS Form 990 asks nonprofits whether they have a written conflict of interest policy, the process they use to manage conflicts, and how they determine whether board members have a conflict of interest. Your state may have additional regulations on conflict of interest, so have the policy and form reviewed by legal counsel to ensure that it meets all relevant regulations. Discuss the conflict of interest policy at a board meeting and customize and amend it as needed. A frank discussion can avoid embarrassing situations down the road. Trustees should read the conflict of interest policy—which identifies its purpose, provides a thorough definition of terms, and outlines procedures for addressing potential conflicts, and violations, if they are determined to exist—before completing the disclosure statement. So that the museum can honestly answer "yes" to the relevant question on IRS Form 990, every member should sign a copy of the disclosure form every year.

The museum's name will automatically be filled in throughout the statement. If the members of the governing body are called something other than "trustees" (such as "directors"), change that throughout the document. Blank forms can be printed from the *Templates for Trustees* website and distributed for trustees to complete and sign, or the administrator can elect to create a form for each member with their name at the top of the form. Remind the board member that the form must be initialed in four places, all questions must be answered, and the form returned to the museum. Make two copies of the signed agreement: one for the trustee and one for the board files.

An annual disclosure of all conflicts of interest should also be completed by members of committees that have board-delegated powers.

TEMPLATE 6B: CONFLICT OF INTEREST POLICY

{[Museum Name]}

Conflict of Interest Policy

For Trustees, Officers, and

Members of Committees with Board-Delegated Powers

Article I—Purpose

1. The purpose of this board conflict of interest policy is to protect {[Museum Name]}'s interests when it is contemplating entering into a transaction or arrangement that might benefit the private interests of an officer or trustee of {[Museum Name]} or might result in a possible excess benefit transaction.

2. This policy is intended to supplement, but not replace, any applicable state and federal laws governing conflicts of interest applicable to nonprofit and charitable organizations.

3. This policy is also intended to identify "independent" trustees.

Article II—Definitions

1. **Interested Person**—Any trustee, principal officer, or member of a committee with governing board-delegated powers who has a direct or indirect financial interest, as defined below, is an interested person.

2. **Financial Interest**—A person has a financial interest if the person has, directly or indirectly, through business, investment, or family:

   a. an ownership or investment interest in any entity with which {[Museum Name]} has a transaction or arrangement,

   b. a compensation arrangement with {[Museum Name]} or with any entity or individual with which {[Museum Name]} has a transaction or arrangement, or

   c. a potential ownership or investment interest in, or compensation arrangement with, any entity or individual with which {[Museum Name]} is negotiating a transaction or arrangement. Compensation includes direct and indirect remuneration as well as gifts or favors that are not insubstantial. A financial interest is not necessarily a conflict of interest. A person who has a financial interest may have a conflict of interest only if the board decides that a conflict of interest exists, in accordance with this policy.

3. **Independent Trustee**—A trustee shall be considered "independent" for the purposes of this policy if he or she is "independent" as defined in the instructions for the IRS 990 form or if the trustee:

   a. is not, and has not been for a period of at least three years, an employee of {[Museum Name]} or any entity in which {[Museum Name]} has a financial interest,

   b. does not directly or indirectly have a significant business relationship with {[Museum Name]}, which might affect independence in decision-making,

c. is not employed as an executive of another corporation where any of {[Museum Name]}'s executive officers or employees serve on that corporation's compensation committee, and

d. does not have an immediate family member who is an executive officer or employee of {[Museum Name]} or who holds a position that has a significant financial relationship with {[Museum Name]}.

Article III—Procedures

1. **Duty to Disclose**—In connection with any actual or possible conflict of interest, an interested person must disclose the existence of the financial interest and be given the opportunity to disclose all material facts to the board.

2. **Recusal of Self**—Any trustee may recuse himself or herself at any time from involvement in any decision or discussion in which the trustee believes he or she has or may have a conflict of interest, without going through the process for determining whether a conflict of interest exists.

3. **Determining Whether a Conflict of Interest Exists**—After disclosure of the financial interest and all material facts, and after any discussion with the interested person, he or she shall leave the board or committee meeting while the determination of a conflict of interest is discussed and voted upon. The remaining board or committee members shall decide if a conflict of interest exists.

4. **Procedures for Addressing the Conflict of Interest**

    a. An interested person may make a presentation at a board or committee meeting, but after the presentation, he/she shall leave the meeting during the discussion of, and the vote on, the transaction or arrangement involving the possible conflict of interest.

    b. The president of the board shall, if appropriate, appoint a disinterested person or committee to investigate alternatives to the proposed transaction or arrangement.

    c. After exercising due diligence, the board shall determine whether {[Museum Name]} can obtain with reasonable efforts a more advantageous transaction or arrangement from a person or entity that would not give rise to a conflict of interest.

    d. If a more advantageous transaction or arrangement is not reasonably possible under circumstances not producing a conflict of interest, the board shall determine by a majority vote of the disinterested trustees whether the transaction or arrangement is in {[Museum Name]}'s best interest, for its own benefit, and whether it is fair and reasonable. In conformity with the above determination, it shall make its decision as to whether to enter into the transaction or arrangement.

5. **Violations of the Conflicts of Interest Policy**

    a. If the board has reasonable cause to believe a member has failed to disclose actual or possible conflicts of interest, it shall inform the member of the basis for such belief and afford the member an opportunity to explain the alleged failure to disclose.

    b. If, after hearing the member's response and after making further investigation as warranted by the circumstances, the board determines the member has failed to disclose an actual or possible conflict of interest, it shall take appropriate disciplinary and corrective action.

Article IV—Records of Proceedings

1. The minutes of the board and all committees with board-delegated powers shall contain:

   a. The names of the persons who disclosed or otherwise were found to have a financial interest in connection with an actual or possible conflict of interest, the nature of the financial interest, any action taken to determine whether a conflict of interest was present, and the board's decision as to whether a conflict of interest in fact existed.

   b. The names of the persons who were present for discussions and votes relating to the transaction or arrangement, the content of the discussion (including any alternatives to the proposed transaction or arrangement), and a record of any votes taken in connection with the proceedings.

Article V—Compensation

1. A voting member of the board who receives compensation, directly or indirectly, from {[Museum Name]} for services is precluded from voting on matters pertaining to that member's compensation.

2. A voting member of any committee whose jurisdiction includes compensation matters and who receives compensation, directly or indirectly, from {[Museum Name]} for services is precluded from voting on matters pertaining to that member's compensation.

3. No voting member of the board or any committee whose jurisdiction includes compensation matters and who receives compensation, directly or indirectly, from {[Museum Name]}, either individually or collectively, is prohibited from providing information to any committee regarding compensation.

Article VI—Annual Statements

1. Each trustee, principal officer and member of a committee with board-delegated powers shall annually sign a statement which affirms such person:

   a. has received a copy of the conflict of interest policy,

   b. has read and understands the policy,

   c. has agreed to comply with the policy, and

   d. understands that {[Museum Name]} is charitable and, in order to maintain its federal tax exemption, it must engage primarily in activities that accomplish one or more of its tax-exempt purposes.

2. Each voting member of the board shall annually sign a statement that declares whether such person is an independent trustee.

3. If, at any time during the year, the information in the annual statement changes materially, the trustee shall disclose such changes and revise the annual disclosure form.

4. The board shall regularly and consistently monitor and enforce compliance with this policy by reviewing annual statements and taking such other actions as are necessary for effective oversight.

Article VII—Periodic Reviews

1. To ensure that {[Museum Name]} operates in a manner consistent with charitable purposes and does not engage in activities that could jeopardize its tax-exempt status, periodic reviews shall be conducted. The periodic reviews shall, at a minimum, include the following subjects:

   a. Whether compensation arrangements and benefits are reasonable, based on competent survey information (if reasonably available) and the result of arm's-length bargaining.

   b. Whether partnerships, joint ventures, and arrangements with management organizations, if any, conform to {[Museum Name]}'s written policies, are properly recorded, reflect reasonable investment or payments for goods and services, further charitable purposes, and do not result in inurement or impermissible private benefit or in an excess benefit transaction.

Article VIII—Use of Outside Experts

1. When conducting the periodic reviews as provided for in Article VII, {[Museum Name]} may, but need not, use outside advisors. If outside experts are used, their use shall not relieve the board of its responsibility for ensuring that periodic reviews are conducted.

TEMPLATE 6C: CONFLICT OF INTEREST DISCLOSURE FORM

{[Museum Name]}

{[Mission Statement]}

Trustee, Officer, and Committee Member

Annual Conflict of Interest Statement

Name:

Date:

Are you a voting trustee? Yes No

Are you an officer? Yes No

If you are an officer, which officer position do you hold?

Do you serve on a committee or task force? Yes No

If yes, which committee or task force?

I affirm the following:
- I have received a copy of the {[Museum Name]} conflict of interest policy. (initial)
- I have read and understand the policy. (initial)
- I agree to comply with the policy. (initial)
- I understand that {[Museum Name]} is charitable and, in order to maintain its federal tax exemption, it must engage primarily in activities that accomplish one or more tax-exempt purposes. (initial)

Disclosures:

Do you have a financial interest (current or potential), including a compensation arrangement, as defined in the conflict of interest policy with {[Museum Name]}?

Yes   No

If yes, please describe it:

If yes, has the financial interest been disclosed, as provided in the conflict of interest policy? Yes No

In the past, have you had a financial interest, including a compensation arrangement, as defined in the conflict of interest policy with {[Museum Name]}? Yes No

If yes, please describe it, including when (approximately):

If yes, has the financial interest been disclosed, as provided in the conflict of interest policy? Yes No

Are you an independent trustee, as defined in the conflict of interest policy? Yes No

If you are not independent, why?

{[Name]}, Board Member

Date

Date of Review by Governance Committee

NOT FOR NEW TRUSTEES ALONE

Neither of these documents is just for new board members. All trustees are required to complete a conflict of interest disclosure each year.

The contract offers an excellent opportunity for current board members to clarify and reaffirm their commitments to the museum. Discuss the document at a full board meeting, and then present it to board members when they renew their terms. If your museum has three-year terms, for example, all trustees will have reviewed their responsibilities, renewed their terms, and signed contracts within three years.

7

Assessing the Process

Template 7: First-Year Board Member Assessment is a survey that new board members complete at the end of their first year of service. It includes multiple-choice as well as open-ended questions (figure 7.7). Both will be useful to the Governance Committee in planning future recruitment and orientation processes.

The best way to learn how a process is working is to ask someone who has been involved. Trustees who have recently joined the board are in the best position to offer useful feedback about recruitment and orientation. At the end of their first year of service, share the link to the survey with all new board members and ask them to answer each question as frankly as possible. Explain that the Governance Committee is not looking for kudos but for constructive criticism it can use to make improvements for the next class of board members. Assure them that their responses will be reported anonymously.

TEMPLATE 7: FIRST-YEAR BOARD MEMBER ASSESSMENT

Unlike Template 2, which is sent to all board members, Template 7 will only be sent to the class of new board members completing their first year of service (not members reelected to subsequent terms). The results will be reported anonymously. Because most incoming classes are small, there is only one report generated from this template: a summary of the distribution of answers and an average score for each question. It is not intended to measure the performance of individual trustees or the board as a whole. (For a complete assessment of the board and the director, see *The Leadership Partnership*, volume 2 in the *Templates for Trustees* series.) The first five sections (questions 1–38 of the survey) are statements related to board-building activities that are rated on a scale from 1 to 4 (with 1 indicating "disagree strongly" and 4 indicating "agree strongly"). The last two sections (questions 39–44) are open-ended questions addressing ongoing board development issues.

As with Template 2, the Governance Committee should review the questions and customize them to the museum and its nominating and orientation process. There are five placeholders at the end for additional questions. However, we suggest keeping the questions consistent from year to year so that the Governance Committee can compare the experience of new board members and track trends over the course of several years.

Report 7: First-Year Assessment

After individual trustees enter their responses to **Template 7: First-Year Board Member Assessment**, the application will automatically generate **Report 7: Survey Responses Tabulation by Member**, with average scores for each statement, for each section, and for the overall board-building process. In general, a score of 3 or higher is a positive sign. If the composite score for any section is above 3, the Governance Committee can assume that

Template 7: First-Year Board Member Assessment Survey

Recruitment

1. The person who contacted me followed up on our initial meeting and stayed in touch throughout the recruitment process.
2. I was invited to the museum to attend exhibitions and special events.
3. I was invited to sit in on a board meeting or committee meeting.
4. I received materials that gave me a good understanding of the museum, its mission, its collection, and its place in the community.
5. I was able to ask questions about the museum, its goals, and its challenges.
6. I received a contract outlining my responsibilities to the museum and the museum's responsibilities to me.
7. I had a clear sense of what kind of time commitment was required.
8. I had a clear sense of financial expectations for board members.

Orientation

9. I received a board manual prior to the orientation meeting.
10. The board manual contained all the information I needed to start serving the museum effectively.
11. The board manual is organized in a way that is useful and easy to update.
12. I attended an orientation meeting for new board members that gave me an understanding of board culture and processes.
13. I was familiarized with the strengths of the collection and had an opportunity to see objects on display and in storage.
14. I was introduced to museum standards and policies on building and caring for the collection.
15. I had an opportunity to meet with the director soon after joining the board.
16. I was introduced to all the staff members with whom I would interact and given a sense of their background and expertise.
17. I was given background information on fellow board members that helped me get to know them.
18. I was introduced to an experienced board member who served as my mentor.
19. I was invited to social gatherings that gave me an opportunity to get to know fellow board members personally.
20. I had a clear understanding of my roles and responsibilities on the board.
21. I was given the opportunity to share information about my interests and experience.

Board Meetings

22. I have received agendas and related materials at least a week prior to meetings.
23. Those presenting information at meetings have been well prepared.
24. Board meetings generally begin and end promptly.
25. The climate at board meetings has allowed different opinions to be expressed and discussed openly.
26. Board meetings put more emphasis on strategic issues than on routine business.
27. Board meetings have been enjoyable; people are able to see the humor in challenging situations.
28. Board meetings make good use of my time.

Board Assignments

29. The board has made good use of my experience and talents from the beginning.
30. I have had opportunities to contribute to a standing committee, ad hoc committee, or task force.
31. My board service has provided me with opportunities to further personal goals and interests.

Communication

32. I have received all the information I've needed to make sound decisions.
33. I have received information in a timely matter, when I've needed it most.
34. Information has been as accurate, concise, and clear as possible.
35. Information has been relevant to my concerns as a trustee.
36. Information has been unbiased, reflecting different perspectives.
37. There has been ample opportunity for dialogue about differing perspectives.
38. Information has been presented in the most effective way (verbal, visual, hard copy, email, etc.).

Continuing Education

39. What would you still like to learn about the intricacies of the museum (such as knowledge of collection areas, behind-the-scenes activities, board committees, or diversity and inclusion initiatives)?
40. What topics could we present in board development sessions that would enhance your ability to contribute to this board (such as fundraising, mission/vision, strategic planning, liability, or financial reports)?
41. What would be the most effective timing and setting for board development sessions?

Board Satisfaction

42. What single thing do you know now that you wish you'd known when you first joined the board?
43. What has been the most rewarding aspect of your board service to date?
44. What has been the least rewarding?

FIGURE 7.1

First-Year Board Member Assessment Report: Question 10 Graph (Courtesy of the Museum Trustee Association)

the process is working relatively well in that area. If the score is between 2 and 3, review the individual statements in that section, looking for specific ways to improve next year. If the score for a particular section is below 2, the Governance Committee should alter the process significantly. Consider one-on-one conversations with board members who completed the survey to learn more about their responses and their suggestions. Better still, invite a new or recent board member to join the Governance Committee. A comparison of the scores in the five sections will reveal the strengths and weaknesses of the current process and help the Governance Committee decide where to allocate resources in the future.

In addition to Report 7, the application graphs responses to each question. The graphs from a survey of a hypothetical board class with four members are shown in figures 7.1–7.6. This hypothetical board has a good board manual (question 10) and has put new members on committees and task forces that are rewarding (question 30). However, this board falls short in other areas. For example, most of the four new members are not happy with the conduct of board meetings (questions 25–28). The Governance Committee could work with the board chair to suggest techniques for planning more efficient meetings, such as consent agendas, and strategies for making discussions more open and productive.

The answers to the six open-ended questions are gathered together, question by question, in **Responses to Open-Ended Questions** (figure 7.7). Though more challenging to interpret, qualitative feedback is every bit as valuable as quantitative. Questions such as "What topics could we present in board development sessions that would enhance your ability to contribute to this board?" or "What single thing do you know now that you wish you'd known when you first joined the board?" often generate meaningful responses.

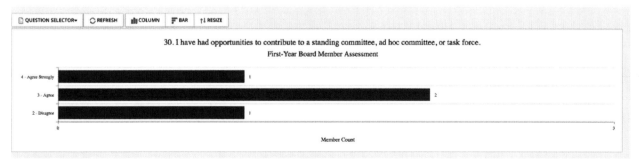

FIGURE 7.2

First-Year Board Member Assessment Report: Question 30 Graph (Courtesy of the Museum Trustee Association)

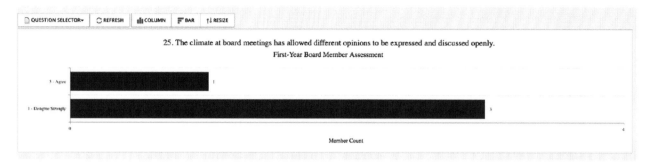

FIGURE 7.3
First-Year Board Member Assessment Report: Question 25 Graph (Courtesy of the Museum Trustee Association)

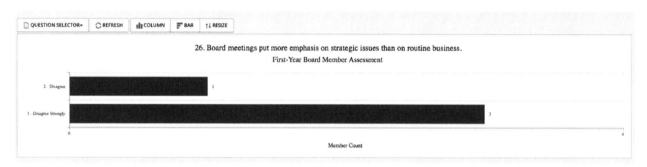

FIGURE 7.4
First-Year Board Member Assessment Report: Question 26 Graph (Courtesy of the Museum Trustee Association)

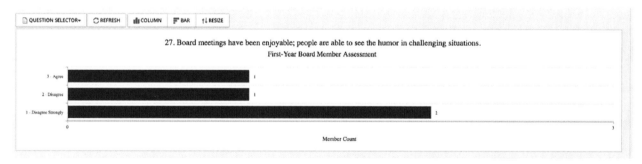

FIGURE 7.5
First-Year Board Member Assessment Report: Question 27 Graph (Courtesy of the Museum Trustee Association)

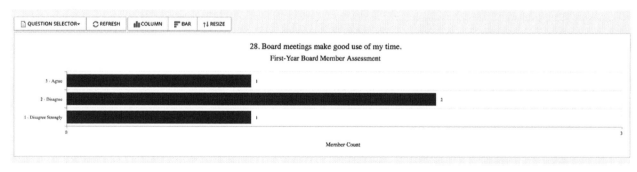

FIGURE 7.6
First-Year Board Member Assessment Report: Question 28 Graph (Courtesy of the Museum Trustee Association)

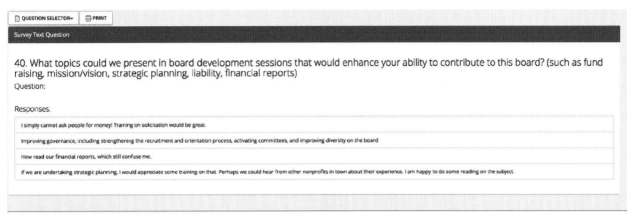

FIGURE 7.7
First-Year Board Member Assessment Report: Responses to Open-Ended Questions (Courtesy of the Museum Trustee Association)

Comparing Scores from Year to Year

The Governance Committee can compare data from year to year to observe trends in recruitment and orientation. Rising overall scores suggest that the committee is making good use of feedback from recent classes of new board members. If overall scores are falling, ask what factors might be contributing to that trend. Has there been a large turnover in the Governance Committee? Have new board classes been larger than usual? Has there been a significant change in practices?

Take Note!

- This survey has been marked "confidential" to encourage honesty. Members of the Governance Committee will be the only people to see the results and individual responses will be reported anonymously.
- The last section focuses on communication, which is key to effective board work. With so many options for communicating these days, the Governance Committee should keep a record of each trustee's preferences for receiving information, including preferred mailing and email addresses and phone numbers. The easier it is for trustees to receive information, the more likely they are to act on it.

8

Orienting New Board Members

THE CORNERSTONE OF BOARD DEVELOPMENT

Mary Baily Wieler, president of the Museum Trustee Association, stresses that the work of the Governance Committee does not end with the nomination and election of new board members: "Orientation is a sound investment in the museum's future. Converting trustees to full engagement in board life is the next step in developing these valuable museum assets."[1] Future board service is built on the introductions and experiences new trustees have in their initial encounters with the museum. The opinions and attitudes they form during their first meetings stay with trustees for many years. To build positive attitudes in new board members, the Governance Committee should:

- establish a welcoming climate by creating opportunities to meet key staff members and volunteers informally,
- provide relevant information and resources where new trustees can find answers to their questions, and
- create early opportunities to become involved in meaningful ways so new board members can immediately play an active role in the work of the board.

Ideally, the orientation session will be scheduled before the first board meeting. Allowing plenty of time for the meeting and incorporating a meal or snack will set a gracious, informal tone and invite an open exchange of ideas. Current board members might call new trustees and ask if they would like to share a ride to the meeting.

Of course, not all trustees join the board at the beginning of the year. For those who join at other times, the outline view of the presentation can guide one-on-one orientation discussions.

Most board orientation sessions focus on the museum, its staff and volunteer structure, and its resources. New trustees also need to learn what it means to be a board member and get a sense of the most critical issues facing the board. But orientation should not just be for new board members. The more current board members attend, the better. This will not only make new members feel welcome but also provide a refresher for longtime members.

Template 8: Orientation

Template 8 is a slide presentation designed to guide the orientation session for the incoming class of board members. This is not a script but a suggested outline to make sure all key issues are covered. It will provide visual talking points for the board and staff members presenting the orientation session and a frame of reference for the new board members attending.

This template is downloaded from the website and customized and saved using PowerPoint. The presentation is in the most vanilla theme available in PowerPoint: sans serif black type on a white background. Switching to a theme, color scheme, and typeface consistent with your museum's graphic identity and brand will connect the presentation with other materials new trustees have received.

The administrator and Governance Committee should endeavor to find facts and data for all of the slides, deleting those that are not relevant and adding slides and images where more detail is desired or required. Most of the information for completing and customizing the orientation presentation already exists and can be gathered from other sources in the museum: the organizational chart, budget, strategic plan, and so forth. There are placeholders in the presentation slides for all of that information, as well as names and photographs of staff and board members and charts summarizing three years of statistics. By inserting the names and photographs of key staff members, the dates of upcoming exhibitions and programs, and other information, the Governance Committee can create a customized slide show. Consider adding other images, particularly to illustrate collections, exhibitions, and programs.

Providing a link to the slide show or printing it as a handout will enable new board members to go back and refresh their memory on topics covered.

This presentation (figure 8.1) includes:

- Slide 1: Title slide, which can be customized with the museum's logo or other images
- Slide 2: A brief history of the museum
- Slides 3–5: The museum's mission, vision, and values
- Slide 6: Highlights from the strategic plan, including major fundraising and program goals
- Slides 7–11: Information about the museum's staff
- Slides 12–13: Information about the museum's volunteers and support groups
- Slides 14–16: An overview of the building and grounds
- Slide 17: Highlights of the collection
- Slides 18–20: A list of upcoming exhibitions and programs
- Slides 21–23: Summaries of membership, attendance, and financial data, tracking performance over three years
- Slides 24–28: A review of the board's duties and responsibilities, including board committees and risk management through insurance
- Slide 29: Examples of recent projects or initiatives that illustrate the proper scope of board oversight
- Slide 30: A summary of major policy and strategy issues on the horizon
- Slide 31: The board calendar for the year, including meetings, fundraisers, and other board events
- Slide 32: Questions

Behind-the-Scenes Tour

The orientation is also an excellent opportunity to provide new trustees with a close-up look at the museum from the inside out. A behind-the-scenes tour might include administrative offices trustees will have occasion to visit, storage areas, conservation facilities, exhibition preparation studios, and registrar's offices. It might also include opportunities to observe a program or tour outside facilities, such as in gardens, grounds, and storage facilities. If there are outreach programs in schools, libraries, or community centers, offer to schedule a group tour or provide details so those who are interested can explore on their own.

Questions and Answers

For new board members, the opportunity to ask questions is one of the most important parts of their orientation. Allow ample time for questions; don't just squeeze in fifteen minutes at the end of the session. Encourage dialogue among all participants: newcomers, veterans, and staff. Invite questions about materials in the board manual

[Museum Name]

New Board Member Orientation

[date]

Museum History

- Founders
- Founding Date
- Original Purpose
- Historical Highlights
- Location(s)

Museum Mission

[mission statement]

Museum Vision

[vision statement if any]

Museum Values

[Values statement or summary if any]

Highlights of the Strategic Plan

[Primary initiatives, goals, strategies]

Staff Organizational Chart

Meet Key Staff Members
Administration

- Director:
  [name]
- Chief Finance Officer:
  [name]
- Assistant Director:
  [name]
- Assistant to Director:
  [name]

Meet Key Staff Members
Development and Membership

- Director of Development:
  [name]
- Director of Membership:
  [name]
- Corporate and Foundation:
  [name]
- Major Gifts Officer:
  [name]

FIGURE 8.1
Board Orientation Presentation (Courtesy of the Museum Trustee Association)

Meet Key Staff Members
Collections

- Chief Curator: [name]
- Collections Manager: [name]
- Curator of Y: [name]
- Curator of X: [name]

Meet Key Staff Members
Education, Exhibitions, Marketing, Technology

- Director of Education: [name]
- Chief Technology Officer: [name]
- Director of Exhibitions: [name]
- Director of Marketing: [name]

Meet Key Volunteers
[volunteer organization name]

- President: [name]
- Special event chair: [name]
- Docent chair: [name]

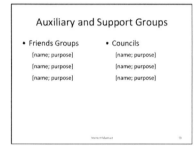

Auxiliary and Support Groups

- Friends Groups
  [name; purpose]
  [name; purpose]
  [name; purpose]
- Councils
  [name; purpose]
  [name; purpose]
  [name; purpose]

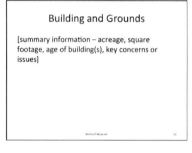

Building and Grounds

[summary information – acreage, square footage, age of building(s), key concerns or issues]

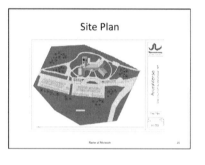

Site Plan

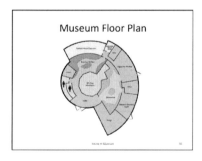

Museum Floor Plan

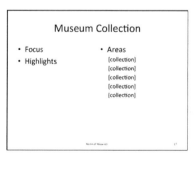

Museum Collection

- Focus
- Highlights
- Areas
  [collection]
  [collection]
  [collection]
  [collection]
  [collection]

Upcoming Exhibitions

[name of exhibition]
[dates]
[highlights]

[name of exhibition]
[dates]
[highlights]

[name of exhibition]
[dates]
[highlights]

[name of exhibition]
[dates]
[highlights]

FIGURE 8.1
(continued)

Programs

- Public Programs
  [Name of Program]
  [Audience]
  [Name of Program]
  [Audience]
  [Name of Program]
  [Audience]
- School Programs
  [Name of Program]
  [Audience]
  [Name of Program]
  [Audience]
  [Name of Program]
  [Audience]

Other Programs

- e.g. Travel/Tour
  - Audience
  - Staff Contact
  - Recent Trips
- e.g. Members Only
  - Audience
  - Staff Contact
  - Recent Programs

Membership

	Current Year	Prior Year	2 Years Prior
Sustaining			
Patron			
Dual/Family			
Individual			
Senior			
Student			

Museum Attendance Profile

	Current Year	Prior Year	2 Years Prior
Regular			
Senior			
Students			
Online			
Offsite			
Special Events			

Museum Financial Profile

	Current Year	Prior Year	2 Years Prior
Operating Revenue			
Investment Revenue			
Total Revenue			
Operating Expense			
Net Revenue			

Primary Board Duties

- Duty of Care: a standard of competence
  - [example]
- Duty of Loyalty: a standard of faithfulness
  - [example]
- Duty of Obedience: a standard of trust
  - [example]

Board Responsibilities

- Stewardship: Staying informed and committed
- Financial Support: Giving and getting
- Leadership: Being an ambassador and connector

Board Organizational Chart

Board Committees

- Executive
- Governance
- Collections
- Building and Grounds
- Development
- Audit
- Finance
- Exhibitions
- Education
- Audience Development
- Personnel
- Planning
- Other (specify)
- Task Force (specify)
- Task Force (specify)

FIGURE 8.1
(continued)

or upcoming issues facing the board. Be up front about board norms so new board members don't need to wonder or learn from their mistakes. Instead, tell them what they need to know so they can fit in and find their place on the board. Include everything from general issues, like "How does this board function?" to specific questions, such as "What do I wear to meetings?" and "Where do I sit?"

MENTORS

Mentoring is a mutual learning experience that expands the perspectives of both new and veteran board members. Pair veteran trustees with new board members, matching them according to shared interests, skills, professional backgrounds, community connections, mutual friends, or personal characteristics.

Once they have had an opportunity to get acquainted, mentors can introduce their new board partners to the rest of the board, providing information about their skills and interests, work experience, family background, travel, and personal qualities. Sharing quotes from conversations with the new trustees or anecdotes from those who recommended them will make the introductions more personal and memorable.

FROM ORIENTATION TO ACTIVATION

After investing so much time, thought, and energy in recruiting and orienting new board members, don't let these assets go to waste. When orientation includes opportunities for new board members to identify their strengths and interests, it leads right into active participation. Share a list of standing committees, task forces, and current board projects, and ask them to indicate their preferences. Then work with committee chairs to make committee assignments, introduce people, and provide orientation. To start contributing to a committee or task force, new board members need to know:

- How the committee's work is related to the museum's mission
- The background and goals of the committee or special project
- Key staff liaisons and their responsibilities
- Schedule of meetings and events
- Information about budget and finances
- Recent issues the committee or task force has addressed
- Upcoming issues

PROVIDE OTHER RESOURCES

Many questions new trustees have can be answered by their mentors, other veteran board members, and staff. But some questions may require a broader background or a specific solution to an unusual challenge. Make sure new board members know about outside organizations that serve trustees' needs (see the final section of the **Resource Guide for** *Building Museum Boards*, page 60). If your board has an institutional membership in any of these organizations, share newsletters with new trustees and encourage them to attend conferences and events. To encourage individuals to join, the Governance Committee should keep an ongoing list of membership information for organizations that support nonprofit governance, inviting board members to add their suggestions.

NOTE

1. Mary Baily Wieler, "Board Education: Making Good Trustees into Great Trustees," *New England Museums Now*, Winter 2015.

Resource Guide for
Building Museum Boards

PUBLICATIONS

BoardSource. "Mentor Your Way to Board Development." Accessed July 26, 2017. https://boardsource.org/wp-content/uploads/2017/07/Mentoring-Board-Development.pdf.

———. "Recommended Governance Practices." Accessed July 26, 2017. https://boardsource.org/wp-content/uploads/2016/10/Recommended-Gov-Practices.pdf.

———. "Using Generative Governance Principles for Better Boardroom Conversations." Accessed July 26, 2017. https://boardsource.org/wp-content/uploads/2017/07/Generative-Governance-Better-Conversations.pdf.

Bobowick, Marla J., Sandra R. Hughes, and Berit Lakey. *Transforming Board Structure: Strategies for Committees and Task Forces*. Washington, DC: BoardSource, 2001.

Calderon, Nancy, and Susan Stautberg. *Women on Board: Insider Secrets to Getting on a Board and Succeeding as a Director*. Ashland, OH: Quotation Media, 2014.

Chait, Richard P., William P. Ryan, and Barbara E. Taylor. *Governance as Leadership: Reframing the Work of Nonprofit Boards*. Washington, DC: BoardSource and John Wiley & Sons, 2005.

Charan, Ram, Michael Useem, and Dennis Carey. *Boards That Lead: When to Take Charge, When to Partner, and When to Stay Out of the Way*. Boston, MA: Harvard Business School Publishing Corporation, 2014.

Dubose, Derwin. "The Nonprofit Sector Has a Ferguson Problem." *Nonprofit Quarterly*, December 5, 2014. Accessed July 26, 2017. https://nonprofitquarterly.org/2014/12/05/the-nonprofit-sector-has-a-ferguson-problem/.

Grace, Kay Sprinkle. *The Ultimate Board Member's Book*. Medfield, MA: Emerson & Church Publishers, 2013.

Houle, Cyril O. *Governing Boards: Their Nature and Nurture*. San Francisco, CA: Jossey-Bass Publishers, 1997.

Hughes, Sandra R., Berit M. Lakey, and Marla J. Bobowick. *The Board Building Cycle: Nine Steps to Finding, Recruiting, and Engaging Nonprofit Board Members*. Washington, DC: BoardSource, 2007.

Ingram, Richard T. *Ten Basic Responsibilities of Nonprofit Boards*, 2nd ed. Washington, DC: BoardSource, 2015.

Katcher, Robin, Susan Gross, Karl Mathiasen, and Neel Master. *Boards Matter: Board Building Tools for the Busy Social Justice Executive*. Washington, DC: Management Assistance Group, 2007. Accessed July 28, 2017. http://www.managementassistance.org/board-building-tools-social-justice.

Lakey, Berit M., Outi Flynn, and Sandra R. Hughes. *Governance Committee*. Washington, DC: BoardSource, 2004.

Lanier, Jim, and E. B. Wilson. *The Governance Committee (Independent Institutions).* Washington, DC: Association of Governing Boards of Universities and Colleges, 2013.

McLaughlin, Thomas A. *Trade Secrets for Nonprofit Managers.* Hoboken, NJ: John Wiley & Sons, 2001.

Mott, William R. *Super Boards.* Self-published, 2014.

Robinson, Maureen. *Nonprofit Boards That Work: The End of One-Size-Fits-All Governance.* Hoboken, NJ: John Wiley & Sons, 2001.

Roche, Nancy, and Jaan Witehead, eds. *The Art of Governance: Boards in the Performing Arts.* New York: Theater Communications Group, 2005.

ORGANIZATIONS

Alliance for Nonprofit Management, 1732 1st Avenue, #28522, New York, NY 10128. Phone: 888-776-2434. Website: www.allianceonline.org.

American Alliance of Museums, 2451 Crystal Drive, Suite 1005, Arlington, VA 22202. Phone: 202-289-1818. Website: www.aam-us.org.

Association of Governing Boards of Universities and Colleges, 1133 20th Street NW, Suite 300, Washington, DC 20036. Phone: 202-296-8400. Website: www.agb.org.

Boardnet USA, a service of the New York Council of Nonprofits, Inc., 272 Broadway, Albany, NY 12204. Phone: 800-515-5012. Website: boardnetusa.org.

BoardSource, 750 9th Street NW, Suite 650, Washington, DC 20001. Phone: 202-349-2580. Website: www.boardsource.org.

CompassPoint Nonprofit Services, 500 12th Street, Suite 320, Oakland, CA 94607. Phone: 510-318-3755. Website: www.compasspoint.org.

Guide Star, 4801 Courthouse Street, Suite 220, Williamsburg, VA 23188. Phone: 757-229-4631. Website: www.guidestar.org.

Independent Sector, 1602 L Street NW, Washington, DC 20036. Phone: 202-467-6161. Website: www.independentsector.org.

Museum Trustee Association, 211 East Lombard Street, Suite 179, Baltimore, MD 21202. Phone: 410-402-0954. Website: www.museumtrustee.org.

National Council of Nonprofits, 1001 G Street NW, Suite 700 East, Washington, DC 20001. Phone: 202-962-0322. Website: www.councilofnonprofits.org.

Nonprofit Risk Management Center, 204 South King Street, Leesburg, VA 20175. Phone: 703-777-3504. Website: www.nonprofitrisk.org.

Appendix

Standing Committees and Ad Hoc Task Forces—Sample Purposes and Responsibilities

AUDIT COMMITTEE

Some museums, particularly larger ones, elect to have an Audit Committee separate from the Finance Committee. Its responsibilities include:

- Interviewing auditors, reviewing bids, and recommending selection of an auditor to the board.
- Receiving the auditor's report, meeting with the auditor, and responding to the auditor's recommendations.
- Assuring compliance with relevant laws and rules affecting accountability, financial reporting, and taxes (some audit committees receive and monitor conflict of interest disclosure forms).

COLLECTIONS COMMITTEE

Unique to museums, the Collections Committee is charged with ensuring the board's stewardship of the museum's most important asset: its collection. The committee works closely with the museum's curatorial staff and frequently includes specialists in the museum's areas of collecting from beyond the board. Its responsibilities are often spelled out in the collections management policy and generally include:

- Approving and recommending to the board the collections management policy.
- Overseeing collections care and security.
- Approving all accessions from the collection or recommending the approval of accessions to the full board.
- Approving all deaccessions to the collection or recommending the approval of deaccessions to the full board; ensuring that deaccessioning is done consistent with the museum's collections management and ethics policies.
- Approving all loans from the collection.

DEVELOPMENT COMMITTEE

The Development (or Fundraising) Committee's job involves more than raising money. The Development Committee is responsible for overseeing the organization's overall fundraising and, in particular, the fundraising done by the board. To accomplish this, its responsibilities are:

- Working with staff to establish a fundraising plan that incorporates a series of appropriate vehicles, such as special events, direct mail, product sales, and so forth.
- Working with development staff in their efforts to raise money.

- Taking the lead in certain types of outreach efforts, such as chairing a dinner/dance committee or hosting fundraising parties, and so on.
- Taking responsibility for involvement of all board members in fundraising, such as having board members make telephone calls to ask for support.
- Monitoring fundraising efforts to be sure that ethical practices are in place, that donors are acknowledged appropriately, and that fundraising efforts are cost-effective.

EXECUTIVE COMMITTEE

Some museums, particularly those with larger or geographically dispersed boards, elect to have an Executive Committee comprising a board chair, other officers, and/or committee chairs. Responsibilities include:

- Overseeing operations of the board, including setting agendas for board meetings and monitoring the work of committees.
- Acting on behalf of the board between meetings.
- Evaluating the work of the director.

FINANCE COMMITTEE

The Finance Committee is generally responsible for:

- Reviewing budgets prepared by staff, helping develop appropriate procedures for budget preparations (such as meaningful involvement by program directors), and ensuring consistency between the budget and the institution's plans.
- Regularly reporting to the board any financial irregularities, concerns, or opportunities.
- Recommending financial policies and guidelines to the board.
- Working with staff to design financial reports and ensure that reports are accurate and timely.
- Overseeing short- and long-term investments (unless there is a separate Investments Committee).
- Recommending selection of the auditor and working with the auditor (unless there is a separate Audit Committee).
- Advising the executive director and business office staff on financial priorities and information systems.

GOVERNANCE COMMITTEE

The Governance Committee is responsible for the health and functioning of the board, including:

- Identifying priorities for board composition.
- Meeting with prospective board members and recommending candidates to the board.
- Recommending a slate of officers to the board.
- Producing reference materials for new board members and conducting orientation sessions.
- Organizing ongoing training sessions for the entire board.
- Creating and circulating board contracts, job descriptions, and conflict of interest disclosure forms.
- Suggesting new, non-board individuals for committee membership.

STRATEGIC PLANNING TASK FORCE

The Strategic Planning Task Force will work with the board and staff of the museum throughout the development of a new strategic plan. Its responsibilities include:

- Structuring an inclusive planning process that connects with staff, visitors, members, and the community.
- Reviewing the organization's current mission, vision, strategic initiatives, major programs, and services.
- Identifying critical strategic issues facing the organization and analyzing strategic options.
- Developing a three- to five-year strategic plan with measurable goals, timetables, and metrics consistent with the professional standards of the American Alliance of Museums.
- Developing a process for the board and staff to monitor progress of the plan and make periodic refinements.

It is anticipated that the work of the Strategic Planning Task Force will be completed between [date] and [date].

[FUNDRAISER] TASK FORCE

The [Fundraiser] Task Force is responsible for the planning, organizing, and implementation of [fundraising event], which is a critical fundraiser and community-building event in the annual calendar. The task force's primary staff contact will be the director of development. Its responsibilities include:

- Creating and monitoring the event's budget.
- Scheduling the time and place of the event.
- Developing the event theme and key messages.
- Identifying and securing the participation of honoree(s).
- Recruiting an honorary chair and host committee of major donors and community leaders and securing their financial commitment.
- Developing a package of sponsorship opportunities and securing sponsorships at every level.
- Working with the museum's graphic designer to develop invitations and all other marketing materials, consistent with the museum's brand.
- Planning and implementing every aspect of the event including decorations, menu, program, and fundraising (table and ticket sales, silent auction, paddle auction, etc.).

The [fundraiser] is generally held in [month or season] and the work of the next year's Task Force begins almost immediately after the event is concluded. The chair(s) of the prior year's event meet with the new Task Force to debrief and share the [fundraiser] planning manual. Because of the complexity of the event, it is advisable to identify the chair(s) one year in advance so that they can participate in planning and implementation as a committee member before assuming the role of chair.

About the Museum Trustee Association and the Authors

The Museum Trustee Association was formed as a committee of the American Association of Museums (now known as the American Alliance of Museums) in 1971. Time revealed that the differences of focus, responsibility, and interest between museum professionals and volunteer boards of trustees would be better served by a separate nonprofit organization. The Museum Trustee Association became a separate entity in 1986 and received its federal IRS 501(c)(3) status in 1991. Since then, MTA has been governed by an elected board of directors representing diverse regions of the United States, the Caribbean, Canada, and Mexico, a variety of museum disciplines and sizes, and wide-ranging areas of expertise in trusteeship. All are current or former museum trustees, and several are founders of MTA.

Daryl Fischer founded Musynergy Consulting in 1993 to provide strategic and interpretive planning, audience evaluation, and board development services to museums and other cultural nonprofits. In 2001 she coauthored the first edition of *Building Museum Boards*, followed by *The Leadership Partnership* (2002), *Executive Transitions* (2003), and *Strategic Thinking and Planning* (2004). Her service on numerous nonprofit boards including the Urban Institute for Contemporary Arts (Grand Rapids, Michigan), the Visitor Studies Association, and the Progressive Women's Alliance of the Lakeshore has given her a profound appreciation for the passion, energy, and expertise that board members bring to the organizations they serve. Her consulting practice has taught her that there is no one-size-fits-all formula for maximizing board effectiveness; however, authentic collaboration with staff and community members leads to a whole that is greater than the sum of the parts. Daryl has an MA from the University of Denver and a BA from Colorado College.

Laura B. Roberts is principal of Roberts Consulting, working with cultural nonprofit organizations on strategic planning, assessment, and organizational development. Laura was executive director of the New England Museum Association and the Boston Center for Adult Education. Previously, she was director of education at three history museums. She is the chair of the Central Square Theater in Cambridge, Massachusetts, and formerly chaired the boards of Tufts University Art Gallery, MassHumanities, and First Night Boston. She teaches museum and nonprofit management at Harvard University Extension, Bank Street College of Education, and Northeastern University. Laura holds an MBA from Boston University Questrom School of Business, an MA from the Cooperstown Graduate Program, and a BA from Harvard University.